BY ROBERT MARKS
PROFILES BY JANET FOX
PHOTO EDITOR JOHN MARKS

PRODUCED IN COOPERATION WITH
THE HIGH POINT HISTORICAL SOCIETY, INC.

Center of High Point's business district, facing south on Main Street, circa 1910. To the left of the trolley car is the *Enterprise* office, and the Elwood Hotel is in the background. *Photo courtesy The High Point Museum Archives.*

Foreword

The High Point Historical Society enters its fourth decade of service as the world prepares for the millennium. Marking the milestones of time creates an opportunity for reflection: to consider the past, its relationship to the present, and its effect on the future.

The High Point Historical Society proudly brings the city's history to life through exhibitions, public programming, and an ever-expanding collection at the High Point Museum & Historical Park. Now, the Historical Society offers a more portable version of High Point's heritage; this book chronicles High Point's growth from a small village to an internationally recognized city, and provides profiles of companies and organizations that have supported its publication.

The history of our city is comprised of more than dates and events. Our heritage resides in the people who have formed High Point's foundation. May their contributions inspire us to assure High Point of a bright future.

On behalf of the High Point Historical Society Board of Trustees, I am honored to present *High Point: Reflections of the Past.*

Vicki S. Dallas
President
High Point Historical Society, Inc.

Preface

After 42 years as a journalist and editor, first with the *High Point Enterprise* and then with *Home Furnishings Daily*, a trade weekly published by Fairchild Publications, I am still amazed at the transformation twice a year of a small city into a worldwide marketing and fashion center for home furnishings. The achievements of the business community as a whole can be traced back to the enduring vision and competitive entrepreneurial spirit of many individuals, and to the cooperative, supportive role of the city. High Point is an American story of success realized through opportunity, faith, commitment, and hard work.

This book is an effort to tell the High Point story from its beginning to the present time as succinctly and accurately as possible. Until now, there has been no one volume that offered such an overview of the city and its people. There are articles that appear in special anniversary issues of newspapers, and there are several compilations into books of official records, personal reminiscences, and profiles of industries. Various accounts of the formation and emergence of the furniture and textile industries in North Carolina, and the South, relate, indirectly, some of the history of High Point. High Point's past is a story of individuals who often were competitors with one another but who could just as often work together toward a common goal and the better welfare of all.

The spirit of seizing opportunity and working for community, so evident in its past, can be a guide for High Point in its future. The vitality of the spirit and the uniqueness of High Point have both been experienced anew in the writing of this book. Over the years I have become familiar with individual and family names prominent in the High Point story, and have listened to many tellings of events and incidents from High Point's past. The writing of this book brought many of those names and events into a closer focus, and a great appreciation for what was accomplished. In this I had the assistance of many resources and the cooperation of many individuals, most of whom are recognized in the Acknowledgements. I am grateful for their support.

Robert Marks

Mann's Drug Store, on South Main Street, circa 1915.
Photo courtesy The High Point Museum Archives.

High Point: Reflections of the Past
Produced in cooperation with the
High Point Historical Society, Inc.
1859 East Lexington Avenue
High Point, North Carolina 27262
(910) 885-6859

By Robert Marks
Editorial Consultant: Robert Hicks
Profiles by Janet Fox
Photo Editor: John Marks

Community Communications, Inc.
Publishers: Ronald P. Beers and James E. Turner

Staff for *High Point: Reflections of the Past*
Publisher's Sales Associate: Robert D. Wills Jr.
Executive Editor: James E. Turner
Managing Editor: Linda Moeller Pegram
Design Director: Camille Leonard
Designers: Melinda Whatley and Rebecca Hockman Carlisle
Layout Editors: Linda M. Pegram, Melinda Whatley and Rebecca H. Carlisle
Production Manager: Corrine Cau
Editorial Assistant: Katrina Williams
Sales Assistant: Annette R. Lozier
Proofreader: Wynona B. Hall
Accounting Services: Sara Ann Turner
Printing Production: Frank Rosenberg/GSAmerica

Community Communications, Inc.
Montgomery, Alabama

James E. Turner, Chairman of the Board
Ronald P. Beers, President
Daniel S. Chambliss, Vice President

© 1996 Community Communications
All Rights Reserved
Published 1996
Printed in the United States of America
First Edition
Library of Congress Catalog Number: 96-44897
ISBN 1-885352-40-9

Every effort has been made to ensure the accuracy of the information herein. However, the authors and Community Communications are not responsible for any errors or omissions which might have occurred.

Table of Contents

Line drawing of the oversized chair by T. Jonathan Willis

Reflections of the Past

Jarrell Hotel at the intersection of today's Main and High Streets. Originally built as a home for Seborn Perry in 1856, it was purchased by Manliff Jarrell, who enlarged it for use as a hotel. This mural was painted on the wall in the home of Mrs. Pauline Simmons Wertz, circa 1960. *Photo courtesy The High Point Museum Archives.*

Chapter One
At First Glance

" *We* are living in a grown up city. High Point is no longer a covert for the wild game of the forests and birds of the air; and as we look back to its infancy we are thrilled with amusing wonder at its magic growth."

—David L. Clark, 1899

D. L. Clark, artist and chronicler of early High Point history. *Photo courtesy of Mary Lib Clark Joyce.*

John Haley, a blacksmith, sheriff, and road commissioner, built this house in 1786 on the Petersburg (Virginia) to Salisbury (North Carolina) Road, a major colonial trade route. The Haley House is the oldest house on its original foundation in High Point. *Photo courtesy The High Point Museum Archives.*

In 1849 the activity in the southwest corner of Guilford County did not in any way resemble a "grown up city." The most significant thoroughfare through the region was the Salisbury Road, which stretched from Petersburg, Virginia, to Salisbury, North Carolina. Its travelers passed through the Quaker community of Jamestown and continued southwestward along a route that would one day be called Lexington Avenue. Along the way were several inns typical of the time, which served as stores and social centers for the local residents, campgrounds for those with their own vehicles, and as hotels for stage riders. In 1818 Jonathan Welch purchased a substantial brick Quaker plan house, which had been constructed by John Haley in 1786 south of Jamestown on Patrick's Creek, and converted it into such an inn. Other hostelries included Towmey's Inn at the intersection with the Cape Fear Road, and Brummell's Inn farther south, just over the Davidson County line. But there was no town . . . .

Though North Carolina had lagged behind most other states in internal development, in 1849 the state legislature overcame regional squabbles between the eastern planters and the "less refined" citizens of the western regions, and chartered both the Fayetteville and Western Plank Road and the North Carolina Railroad Company. This combination would prove to be the impetus for High Point.

When completed in 1853, the Fayetteville and Western Plank Road had a surface of three-inch thick oak planks on a base of pine logs. The charter required 100 feet of right-of-way and 10 feet of width. The 129-mile "Appian Way of North Carolina" is reputed to have been the longest of its kind in the world. The plank road was intended to connect Fayetteville and the Cape Fear River with Salisbury in the central Piedmont. However, the Salem community in Forsyth County successfully lobbied to become the ultimate destination, haply bringing it through the southwest corner of Guilford County along the route of the old Cape Fear Road.

The North Carolina Railroad was to link the Wilmington and Weldon Railroad at Goldsboro in the east with Charlotte in the southwest corner of the Piedmont via

Raleigh, Greensboro, Lexington, and Salisbury. The state government promised $2 million to finance the railroad if private investors raised another $1 million. The course was to be surveyed in four sections, with the third section stretching from the eastern Guilford County line to Lexington. The three possible routes considered for this section were designated as the "Fair Grove, middle, and Northern line." The third section engineers were under the supervision of J. L. Gregg. Their survey indicated that the middle line just west of the intersection of railroad with the soon-to-be-constructed plank road was, at 940 feet above sea level, the highest point in elevation along the entire route. On the advice of the chief engineer, the directors adopted this middle route.

Legend has it that "Cap'n" Gregg coined the name for a future city when he proclaimed, "This is the highest point along the whole survey, so we will mark it *high point*."

In 1853, with the completion of the plank road to Salem and the arrival of the railroad a certainty, business-minded individuals began to see the unique opportunity that the crossing of important trade arteries could afford. The woods and farmland around the junction were owned by Thomas Sechrest, Solomon Kendall, and Nathan Johnson, and each began dividing and selling his property. Through fliers and other advertisements, word spread that "town lots [were] for sale on each side of the Plank Road . . . in a healthy country." One of the first transactions involved the purchase of 94 acres from Johnson by Dr. R. C. Lindsay. Dr. Lindsay then purchased six acres from Kendall near the crossroads, and constructed a home. Kendall also sold property to William Welch and to Francis Fries. Welch promptly divided

his nearly 12 acres into lots, which he then advertised for sale "at High Point." He promised potential buyers that "the location is healthful and promises fair to become one of the most thriving towns on the entire line of railroad." Fries, a Salem resident, constructed a warehouse to service both the wagons loaded with goods traveling the plank road and the freight which the railroad would bring. In October, Seborn Perry purchased two lots in the southwest corner of the intersection for $182.

Stores and other buildings were springing up around the intersection, transforming the junction into a thriving community. Goods, particularly farm products, moved in and out of warehouses, and up and down the lines. A small barrel-making operation was started. By far the most prosperous pursuit was that of a merchant, and several general stores were opened. In one such store, that of William Welch, a U.S. Post Office opened on December 19, 1854. This required the official naming of the village, and after some debate, "High Point" became the approved designation. Austin, William Welch's son,

"Cap'n" J. L. Gregg driving the stake marking the "high point" of the North Carolina Railroad. *Photo courtesy The High Point Museum Archives.*

was the first postmaster. The first railroad cars pulled into the new station on November 22, 1855, as a crowd gathered by the tracks to watch and cheer. By June of 1857, the hub was already the fourth highest revenue producer on the entire rail line. A voting precinct was established for the area that year and an election held in which 159 votes were cast. The next year a total of 226 votes were counted in a second contest. The population for the precinct in 1859 totaled 596, including slaves and freedmen.

A community was taking shape. And the people were of a religious nature. The first recorded meetings were of a Sunday school organized by Margaret Denny, and the town's first sermon came from a Methodist itinerant, Reverend Peter Doub, in 1856. Since there was no church, the worshipers made a pulpit from "an old goods box, rolled out into the woods." The Methodists completed a building two years later. They, in turn, shared with the Presbyterians who had a minister but no church, a condition which they rectified the following year. Also in 1859, a Baptist congregation moved their assembly from the Jamestown area, renaming themselves the High Point Missionary Baptist Church.

The time had come to officially make High Point a town. At a meeting held in Sewell Farlow's store in early 1859, the decision was made to petition the North Carolina Legislature for a charter incorporating the village. Accordingly, the state legislature granted the charter on May 26, 1859. The boundaries were "to be one mile North, South, East, and West from the crossing where the Fayetteville and Western Plank Road crosses the North Carolina Rail Road in said town making a square of two miles."

Seborn Perry, early merchant and landowner.
Photo courtesy The High Point Museum Archives.

The charter also contained a directive, at the request of the populace, that no "spirituous liquors" were to be sold. A board of five commissioners, each to serve a term of one year, was appointed consisting of John Carter, Eli Denny, Sewell Farlow, Dr. Robert C. Lindsay, and Jeremiah Piggott. They held their first meeting on July 28, 1859, in Farlow's store, electing Dr. R. C. Lindsay chairman, and approving a tax rate of one cent per $100 valuation, with a poll tax of 20 cents. Gambling was outlawed and fines set for obstructing the streets and disturbing the peace. In the first election the following February, Nathan Hunt Jr. was voted the first mayor.

The citizens of the new town soon had a newspaper of their own. The first issue of the High Point *Reporter*, edited by James H. Moore, appeared on January 12, 1860. A glance through the pages of the weekly paper revealed a burgeoning mercantile center. Seven "dry goods" stores, an attorney, an architect, a doctor, a dentist, a tailor, a jeweler, and several craftsmen advertised in its pages, along with a "picture gallery" of local artist D. L. Clark. There were already two hotels. The Laurence House was converted from the home which Seborn Perry had constructed on the southwest corner of the main intersection, and Jeremiah Piggott had constructed a "large brick hotel" farther south on the rail line. Optimism abounded. Said D. L. Clark, "Everything was looking bright and promising when a blighting change fell upon us: The token of war had been sounded."

The coming of the Civil War was both

The main portion of Jarrell's Hotel, owned by Manliff Jarrell, was Seborn Perry's original residence.
Photo courtesy The High Point Museum Archives.

Bellevue Hotel, formerly the Barbee Hotel, which was used as a hospital during the Civil War. *Photo courtesy The High Point Museum Archives.*

boom and bane for High Point. Though a considerable amount of sentiment for the Union existed west of the sandhills region of North Carolina, most Tarheels followed their kindred spirit and supported the Southern cause. Because of its location on two major transport routes, the town became a staging area and supply point. Several factories manufactured small arms, gunstocks, hats, and other items beneficial to the war effort. Both freight and passengers increased dramatically on the rail line. Manliff Jarrell, who purchased the Laurence House in 1863, threw up addition after addition trying to keep up with demand. During the first year of the war, North Carolina regiments were trained at a state military facility, Camp Fisher, three-fourths of a mile northeast of the train depot, named for Colonel Charles F. Fisher, president of the North Carolina Railroad. Fisher

had been among the first to be killed at the first Battle of Manassas. Camp Fisher was abandoned in November 1861.

During the later years of the war, High Point began to see the ugly side of war. William Barbee had purchased the three-story brick hotel after the death of Jeremiah Piggott in late 1859. Governor Zebulon Vance agreed in 1863 to exempt Barbee from military service so long as he maintained his establishment as "an open house for wounded soldiers." In the early months of 1865 the conflict finally reached central North Carolina. After the battle of Bentonville, near Smithfield, an unprecedented stream of wounded poured into High Point, forcing the creation of makeshift hospitals in every possible location. It also brought another enemy, smallpox, forcing the operation of a "pest house" on the outskirts of town.

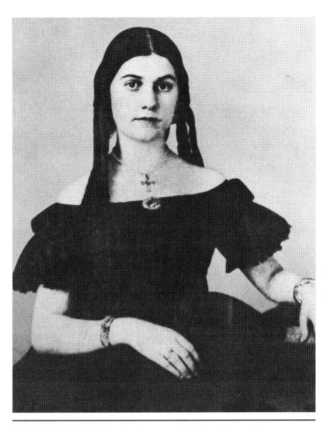

Laura Wesson, heroine of the "pest house."
Photo courtesy The High Point Museum Archives.

At its onset, the editor of the *Reporter* had acknowledged the calamity that war could bring, but hoped that the new village might "evade its force." Though it had made it through nearly four years without episode, the town was not to be left unscathed. A Union military force arrived in High Point on April 10, 1865. The cavalry brigade of Colonel William J. Palmer was part of General George Stoneman's command, which had left Morristown, Tennessee, about a month before to raid into western North Carolina and southwestern Virginia. The objective was to burn supplies, cut rail lines, and destroy bridges behind the retreating Confederate armies. Palmer's troopers burned the depot and several warehouses near the station. The fires threatened Barbee's "hospital," which was saved by pouring water over long cloths stretched across the eaves.

Though the war was officially ended within days, the hospitals of High Point remained full. The people of the town continued to minister to the sick and wounded. One such attendant was 19-year-old Laura Wesson, a Virginian whose journey to Charleston, South Carolina, had been interrupted by the presence of the Federal Army. Knowing the risk of smallpox infection, she still chose to aid those forced to the "pest house." Ironically, she became High Point's most famous heroine when she herself succumbed to the disease.

With the end of the war, High Point, like much of the South, was destitute. Though the citizens hoped for a swift recovery, it was not to be, and most were forced to provide for themselves. However, Quakers in northern and midwestern states, aware of conditions among Friends in North Carolina,

Captain John Sloan of the Guilford Grays, a volunteer company of infantry which was commissioned on March 15, 1860. The company later engaged in 20 battles during the Civil War, 1861-65.
Photo courtesy The High Point Museum Archives.

Dr. A. J. Sapp, Civil War physician and civic leader. He tended to smallpox victims and survived the epidemic that claimed Laura Wesson's life.
Photo courtesy The High Point Museum Archives.

formed the Baltimore Association in 1865 to launch a program of relief. In that first winter after the war, they focused their efforts on provision of food and clothing. Over the next seven years, the Association provided assistance for the repair of homes and buildings, the restoration of Meeting Houses, and the opening of schools. A major effort was the "Model Farm," created on the Nathan Hunt farm in the Springfield community for the purpose of demonstrating and implementing new farming methods to boost the land's productivity.

The manufacturing operations which supported the Confederate war effort were now defunct, and the war had forced the *Reporter* out of business. The paper's press was sold to satisfy a debt. Business for the shops and stores of the village was virtually nonexistent as their customers struggled to rebuild their own livelihoods. With the railroad devastated, commerce was at a standstill.

But 1868 brought a brighter outlook, and a new vision. The railroad had, for the most part, been restored, and in April the city subscribed $10,000 toward the completion of the western North Carolina line through Asheville and into Tennessee. Merchants were beginning to recover, but the war had left a feeling that "back country trade was too uncertain." A decade after its formation, the population of the town was nearly unchanged. Several "progressive citizens" had observed that industry, like that in the northern states, provided a stable base for growth. Seeing an opportunity, D. L. Clark, Dr. A. J. Sapp, and Seborn Perry formed a "committee" to pay a visit to a Yankee industrialist who was registered at the Barbee Hotel.

William Henry Snow had recently moved to Greensboro from Dracut, near Lowell, Massachusetts, for the health of his wife, Lydia. Serving as a first lieutenant in the Sixth Massachusetts Regiment, he had spent the later years of the Civil War in North Carolina, and had been impressed by the moderate climate. After the move, he discovered an abundance of several fine-grain

Model Farm House on the Nathan Hunt farm. *Photo courtesy The High Point Museum Archives.*

woods, persimmon and dogwood in particular, which might replace the expensive apple wood used for shuttle blocks in northern textile mills. With the help of friends back in Lowell, he opened a shuttle factory in Greensboro. Perry promised capital if Snow would move the operation to his town. Although it took four years to accomplish the task, it was described as "a bright day" when the partners "blew the first whistle that signaled the coming of the manufacturing prosperity."

D. L. Clark reported that "car after car was being shipped filled with spokes, handles, and shuttle blocks"; but less than a year after the opening, the Greensboro *Patriot* reported the factory "totally consumed by fire." With less insurance than investment, Seborn Perry opted out of the arrangement,

but Snow, who had achieved the affectionate rank of "Captain," was not deterred and quickly rebuilt the business. This modest beginning provided the example. The little village was about to experience its own industrial revolution.

By the 1880s others were joining Captain Snow in manufacturing enterprises. A. A. Barker & Sons made dressed lumber products like doors and sashes. Seborn Perry decided the spoke and handle business might be profitable after all, and opened a factory of his own. The town's first textile operation was a cotton mill, Willowbrook Manufacturing, founded by Oliver S. Causey in 1880. Though it burned to the ground in 1884, Causey was joined by a partner, E.H.C. Field, and reopened the shop as the Empire Cotton and Plaid Mill. It ran "night

Captain William Henry Snow, early industrialist.
Photo courtesy The High Point Museum Archives.

Reflections of the Past

The Modern Tobacco Barn was designed by Captain William Henry Snow to improve the curing of tobacco.
Photo courtesy The High Point Museum Archives.

and day," and owned 18 houses "filled with families . . . connected with the mill." There were three mineral distributors—Armfield Gold and Copper, Ferrabee Gold and Copper, and Lindsay Gold and Copper. These were the result of numerous mining operations which stretched from the northeast to southwest of the town.

Tobacco was becoming big business in the village. Three factories, A. H. Lindsay and Company, W. P. Pickett and Company, and Welborne and Company, produced chewing tobacco and cigars with names like "Queen of Sumatra," "Legal Tender," and "Pride of North Carolina." The Pickett company endured until 1905, when it was sold to R. J. Reynolds of Winston-Salem. There were also several large warehouses where the golden leaf was bought and sold. Captain Snow, too, had an interest in tobacco. He patented a new method of curing, and formed the Modern Tobacco Barn Company with three Philadelphia businessmen. Restless to pursue other business directions, he divided the woodworking business, giving the lumber mill to his son, Ernest A. Snow, and the spoke and handle enterprise to his son-in-law, J. Elwood Cox. An 1887 article by the Charlotte *Chronicle* reported 500 persons employed in factories, and called the Snow Lumber Company "the biggest woodworkers in North Carolina." The *Chronicle* proclaimed, "It will pay anyone traveling through North Carolina to stop over at High Point and visit her manufactories."

By the spring of 1882 the town once again had its own newspaper. Though two other weeklies had failed since the end of the Civil War, the *Pioneer*, founded by Edwin D. Steele, would be a permanent fixture. The paper changed hands five times before 1886, becoming the *Farm and Fireside*, and finally the *Enterprise*.

Growth pointed to the need for a local financial institution. The National Bank of High Point was the first such enterprise, opening in May 1886. Later, its prosperity would be attributed to a policy of "large cash reserves to accommodate depositors without inconvenience." The following year an "interesting and enthusiastic meeting of citizens" was held in one of the tobacco warehouses "to organize a Building and Loan Association."

The town was still quite small. Every major shop and factory was within a quarter mile of the railroad depot. Everything was within walking distance, the most common form of travel. Shops lined what was coming to be called "Main Street" for several blocks north and south of its intersection with the rail line. A "crossing station" protected the citizenry from the numerous trains passing through the town each day. The streets themselves were dirt, or mud, depending upon the weather, and their condition was often a source of complaint to the town's commissioners. To combat the potential for fire, an ordinance was passed outlawing wooden buildings in the business section. The district already boasted of two "solid blocks" of brick stores. There was a housing shortage in the 1880s as the population more than doubled, to over 2,000, and several farms near downtown began to be subdivided into lots for new homes.

High Pointers of the late nineteenth century entertained themselves in various ways. Parties, balls, suppers, and "bazaars" were common distractions. These functions centered on the town's halls. The most famous of

The National Bank of High Point, the city's first bank.
Photo courtesy The High Point Museum Archives.

J. Elwood Cox, manufacturer, banker, and
builder of the Elwood Hotel.
Photo courtesy The High Point Museum Archives.

Bertha Snow Cox, daughter of Captain W. H.
Snow and wife of J. Elwood Cox.
Photo courtesy The High Point Museum Archives.

Mr. and Mrs. Tom Thumb appeared at Jarrell's Hall.
Photo courtesy The High Point Museum Archives.

REV. WAH HOCHE,

525252525252525252525252752525252

The Indian will give an Entertainment to-
night at

Jarrell's Hall.

Everybody is invited to come out to the
above-named hall where you will have the
pleasure of seeing some of the manners and
customs of the Apapchee Indians,

Such as the War Instruments, Moccasins,
Bow, Arrows and Quivers, Buck Skins,
Head Dress Pachetly, Buffalos, the
Indian War dance and many other
wonderful sights.

Admission   -   -   -   10 cents.

Doors open at 7:30 o'clock; commence at 8.

For the benefit of the Church.

Handbill for entertainment at Jarrell's Hall.
Photo courtesy The High Point Museum Archives.

these was Jarrell's Hall, an appendage of
Jarrell's Hotel. It advertised a "stage appropri-
ate for theatrical troupes and exhibitions of
all kinds—Will seat 500 persons comfort-
ably." Many gatherings, particularly those of
a public nature, were held in the large tobacco warehouses. Social organizations included
The Lyceum Club, "the social and literary
light of the community," and a chapter of the
Women's Christian Temperance Union. Since
the articles of incorporation already prohibit-
ed the sale of alcohol, the group concentrated
its efforts on the flow of illegal liquor into
the town.

There were two more churches created in
the 1880s. The Saint James Episcopal
Mission was organized in 1882 in the home
of a parishioner. Through the efforts of the
Springfield Meeting, the Quakers formed the
High Point Monthly Meeting the next year.
The building which they constructed also
came to be used as the site of the North
Carolina Yearly Meeting. And by 1888, all
but the Presbyterians had services every week.
Common to this period was the "protracted
meeting," nightly services held in various
locations, often the combined effort of several denominations, and many times lasting for
a month or more. During the summer
months the merchants would fill their shelves
for "camp meeting trade" as visitors passed
through the town on their pilgrimages to
nearby meetings.

Schools were not as easy to come by as
churches. With no public education system,
local schools were not guaranteed to survive
from year to year. North Carolina instituted a
"free school" system for each county following the Civil War. This established five
schools in the township, but none near the
town, so "subscription" schools were usually
held in the home of concerned townswomen.
In 1883 the citizens passed a referendum
providing partial funds for "nine months
continuous school."

In spite of its notoriety as an industrial
center, High Point gained a reputation as
a vacation and health resort. Newspaper

Quaker meeting house of the High Point Monthly Meeting and North Carolina Yearly Meeting, at Church and Lindsay Streets.
Photo courtesy The High Point Museum Archives.

advertisements had long claimed benefits from "salubrious air, quiet and cheap living," and even a mineral spring with "healing properties" to attract visitation. Report was also made that during one 13-month span there was no recorded death except "two or three enfants," and that there were only three deaths of persons between 15 years and 40 years of age over a four-year period. Touted for its accommodations at the Jarrell and Bellevue Hotels, its appealing countryside, and its "pure" freestone water, High Point was the only North Carolina community listed in the 1892 publication *Health Resorts of the South.*

The lure of accommodations, mild climate, access to the railroad, plus a countryside teeming with quail and ducks also brought people, particularly wealthy Northerners, to High Point for social rest, relaxation, and recreation. The Eastern Field Trials Club moved its sporting events from Robbins Island in Peconic Bay, Long Island, to High Point in 1882. By the turn of the century, a string of hunting lodges and game preserves stretched in an arc around High Point, from the Deep River in the east through Randolph County to the south into Davidson County on the west. Among the most prominent of these hunting preserves were those of Pierre Lorillard, the tobacco magnate; Clarence Mackay, president of the Postal Telegraph Company; W. Gould Brokaw, grandson of Jay Gould; George Jay Gould, another heir to the Gould railroad fortune; and William Ziegler, a New York real estate developer. Mackay employed architect Stanford White to design and build the lodge on his park. Brokaw's Fairview Park Estate was a low, white structure 160 feet in length with 15 bedrooms, a gun room, library, gymnasium, shooting gallery, and squash court. Also at Fairview Park were a racetrack, stables, kennels, and cottages for the gamekeepers and trainers. Such attractions brought a steady stream of celebrities, politicians, and businessmen to High Point into the early twentieth century.

Industrial growth in High Point mirrored

many small towns throughout the South. The diverse development was nothing spectacular, but it offered the citizenry a promise of prosperity. Even in these early years, some recognized the town's potential. The Charlotte *Chronicle* had described High Point as "the most important manufacturing town on the North Carolina Railroad." That was the beginning of the town's fame. By the turn of the century, D. L. Clark could write, "Though she once 'crawled' she can now stand alone. We are proud of our young city." ☜

A High Point hunting party. *Photo courtesy The High Point Museum Archives.*

Interior of the lodge at Fairview Park, the estate of W. Gould Brokaw.
Photo courtesy The High Point Museum Archives.

Berta Margarite Lindsay and Andrew Lindsay, circa 1898, children of Mary Sapp and John A. Lindsay.
John Lindsay was cofounder of Eagle Furniture Company and a city alderman.
Photo courtesy The High Point Museum Archives.

Furniture Manufacturers Exposition Building, circa 1915. *Photo courtesy The High Point Museum Archives.*

Chapter Two
A Familiar View

Main Street was decorated with bunting and flags. The townspeople streamed in to get their first look at a building that would change the course of the city forever.

Interior of Amos Furniture Company's Store.
Photo courtesy The High Point Museum Archives.

Cover of 1908 book by J.J. Farriss promoting High Point.
Photo courtesy The High Point Museum Archives.

There was little doubt that this would finally be the culmination of a 20-year effort to become a marketing center. Luncheons were planned, automobiles were rented to provide transportation from nearby towns, and citizens offered sleeping quarters in their homes, for the number of visitors was expected to far exceed the usual accommodations. Everywhere they went, buyers would be greeted with the slogan "Oh Boy! You're in the Furniture Town Now!"

The successful opening of the Southern Furniture Exposition Building in June 1921 was a defining moment for High Point. It completed the framework of both factories and showrooms with which its modern citizens have become so familiar. Before 1889, this town with around 2,000 residents counted among its principal businesses the usual endeavors found in a New South "industrial" village. By the end of the First World War, with a population of over 15,000, the textile industry had developed such a presence that the town would soon claim to be "The Hosiery Capital of the World." Still, furniture would ultimately be responsible for the city's distinctive character. With over 40 such plants, High Point was already the leading furniture manufacturer in the South when the first buyers passed the threshold of the new market center.

The transformation of this "little idle hamlet" at the junction of a railroad and a thoroughfare into a manufacturing and marketing center in three decades was the accomplishment of friends who were intense competitors as well. Their entrepreneurial drive was fueled by the energy of their ambitions and a vision of prosperity in opportunity. Men with unlikely backgrounds found success in their innate abilities, and forged first an industrial foundation, and then a marketing strategy for its goods. Their legacy brought benefits to the citizens of this "little city" long after their time.

E. A. Snow frequently called on northern customers, as demand for lumber there was high, and one such trip to a furniture

Ernest Ansel Snow, son of Captain W.H. Snow and
cofounder of the High Point Furniture Company.
Photo courtesy The High Point Museum Archives.

John H. Tate, cofounder of the
High Point Furniture Company.
Photo courtesy The High Point Museum Archives.

Thomas Franklin Wrenn, cofounder of the
High Point Furniture Company.
Photo courtesy The High Point Museum Archives.

Fred N. Tate, president of Continental Furniture Company and mayor
of High Point from 1909 to 1915.
Photo courtesy The High Point Museum Archives.

establishment in Baltimore changed the future of High Point. There he noticed the sharp difference in price between the raw lumber and the finished product. He returned home with an idea. One February day in 1889, in a rear office of the Jarrell Hotel, Snow met with John H. Tate and Thomas F. Wrenn to organize High Point Furniture Company with a capital investment of $9,000. Tate and Wrenn each invested $3,000, almost the entire life savings of each at the time. For his share, Snow furnished the lumber for construction of the factory and manufacture of the furniture. A small factory building two stories high, measuring 40 feet by 80 feet, was constructed, and a starting labor force of 25 to 50 men were hired. The first piece they manufactured was a desk for the office of the new company and remained the only piece of furniture there for some time.

High Point Furniture was an immediate success. The company sold single beds to retailers for 75 cents and three-piece bedroom suites, including bed, dresser, and washstand, for $7.50. A dividend was declared after the company's first year of operation when sales totaled $75,000. Sales doubled within the second year. By the end of the decade, High Point Furniture Company employed 85 workers and offered 20 styles of bedroom furniture to retailers.

Such success transformed High Point. Described in 1887 as the "world's greatest source" of shuttle blocks and bobbins, and as the "most important manufacturing town on the North Carolina Railroad" for its textiles, woodworking, and tobacco factories, by 1898 the town was being compared with Grand Rapids, Michigan, the premiere furniture production center in the country. Despite warnings that the community could support only one such plant, Snow Lumber executive R. F. Dalton joined forces with O. C. Wysong, the superintendent of High Point Furniture, to form Guilford Furniture Company in the summer of 1890. Also that year, J. B. Best and R. J. Lindsay organized

Elwood Hotel on Main Street, built in 1903 by J. Elwood Cox. *Photo courtesy The High Point Museum Archives.*

the first seating business, High Point Chair Company. With two more furniture interests thriving, the floodgates were opened. By 1896 the list had grown to nine firms, adding Tate Furniture and Eagle Furniture in 1893; Alma Furniture in 1895; and three— Southern Chair, Globe Furniture, and High Point Upholstery—in 1896. One of the largest of the new furniture manufacturers, Globe Furniture Company was organized with a capital investment of $40,000 by Dr. W. G. Bradshaw, a medical doctor; J. E. Cartland, a dentist; and J. Elwood Cox.

What had brought such tremendous success so quickly? Timing and several key ele-

ments made High Point the "Grand Rapids of the South." Obviously, being located on the rail line offered businesses an efficient means for distributing their products, but three other tangible reasons allowed the town to advance beyond its local limitations. First, manufacturers had to increase the volume of lumber which could be reaped from the surrounding countryside. In 1887 at least 50 wagons of oak, hickory, walnut, and persimmon were brought to town each day; but, to support more woodworking industry, additional supplies were needed. A rail line to Asheboro, 20 miles to the southeast, had been in the talking stages for several years.

31

Captains of

F.M. Pickett, founder of Pickett's Tobacco Factory.
Photo courtesy The High Point Museum Archives.

Manliff Jarrell Wrenn, High Point Furniture Company.
Photo courtesy The High Point Museum Archives.

J.P. Redding, Alma Furniture Company.
Photo courtesy The High Point Museum Archives.

Industry

R.F. Dalton, Snow Lumber Company.
Photo courtesy The High Point Museum Archives.

Alexander M. Rankin, Rankin Coffin and
Casket Company, and president of several
furniture companies.
Photo courtesy The High Point Museum Archives.

Dr. J.J. Cox, Home Furniture Company.
Photo courtesy The High Point Museum Archives.

Pickett Cotton Mill. *Photo courtesy The High Point Museum Archives.*

W. H. Snow had even started the project with his own money around 1883. However, the project was not successful until the state legislature approved the sale of bonds by the town to raise the capital to finish it. Completed in late 1888, the new line allowed vast amounts of lumber to be hauled via rail.

Two other factors which aided the development of industry in High Point were an abundant supply of cheap labor resulting from the displacement of farmworkers, and the general return of prosperity which allowed Southerners to buy new furniture.

Perhaps the most important factor in the commencement of the furniture industry in the city, however, was the town's businessmen. These men with imagination, ability, drive, and "pluck" were amazingly able to raise most of the capital for their ventures locally, and the profits from one were often used to begin another. Appearing again and again as officers and investors are the names E. A. Snow, Thomas F. Wrenn, M. J. Wrenn, John H. Tate, Albert E. Tate, R. F. Dalton, J. B. Best, R. J. Lindsay, J. J. Cox, J. Elwood Cox, Alexander M. Rankin, F. M. Pickett, W. H. Ragan, Jonathan P. Redding, Henry W. Fraser, T. H. Patten, J. E. Cartland, Percy V. Kirkman, and J. J. Welch. Among them were seven merchants, three textile manufacturers, three lumbermen, four doctors, a dentist, a

J.J. Farriss, editor and publisher of the *Enterprise*.
Photo courtesy The High Point Museum Archives.

railroad conductor, an insurance agent, a tobacco manufacturer, and a teacher.

The *Enterprise* reported that High Point was "imbued with the manufacturing spirit." Its latest owner, J. J. Farriss, must be credited with the major role in fostering such vigor. He was the city's greatest promoter. Arriving in High Point at the invitation of his brother, Charles, they purchased the paper in 1888, declaring it would "give the news and encourage the manufacturing spirit in the community." When his brother moved on two years later, Farriss provided ample advertisement of the opportunities for both potential investors and laborers through the *Enterprise* and regular publications of a

booster book entitled *High Point, N.C.: A Brief Summary.* "One factory followed another in rapid succession," he asserted in 1896 with an obvious note of pride in what had been accomplished, "and to-day over one thousand artisans are responding to the music of twenty whistles." As the century turned, high profits with few failures encouraged rapid expansion. From 1901 to 1903, 22 new companies were launched, many in furniture accessories such as bedding, glass, mirrors, and excelsior (packing materials).

Successful as manufacturers, the leaders of the town's new furniture concerns faced the challenge of outside competition and the need to appeal to more customers. Business

High Point Overall Company. *Photo courtesy The High Point Museum Archives.*

leaders sought ways of cooperation to break this cycle and gain customers in national markets. Manufacturers improved quality and started showing their products at markets in New York, Chicago, and Grand Rapids. The idea to have a market, or "exposition," in High Point also gained support. Farriss believed that furniture makers needed a common voice, so in April 1901, together with two out-of-town trade journalists, he started the *Southern Furniture Journal.* In December, 35 men voted to back a "Southern Furniture Exposition," but the plan never materialized. In an attempt to avoid "flooding" their markets, 27 companies from across the state joined forces in 1902 to create the North Carolina Furniture Manufacturers' Association. The following year, 21 local leaders organized the

"Manufacturers Club" to bolster the growth and image of the city.

Just over half of the city's factories were furniture firms; the others were a diverse mixture ranging from silk to streetcars. One industry with its beginnings in this period, however, would leave an indelible mark on the town. J. Henry Millis and J. H. Adams had established a business relationship in 1901 as partners in High Point Overall Company. Adams saw an opportunity to combine the sales of the overalls with hosiery, and pitched the idea to his associate. Having "great faith in Mr. Adams," Millis agreed to join him in founding a second High Point hosiery mill. Securing the efforts of an experienced superintendent, C. C. Robbins of Randleman, the new endeavor would be significantly more successful than the original operation by that name, which had failed nine years before.

Until 1905, the town's workers and the factory owners had mostly seen eye to eye. J. J. Farriss had reported in 1903 that "the labor problem" which had affected the major industrial centers of the nation, in High Point was "not a problem." But as a result of union organizations that began the previous year, 1906 brought the city its own labor dispute, dubbed the "High Point Lockout" by journalists across the state. Manufacturers claimed it resulted from "out side influence" and "agitators … recently come to High Point," while union leaders believed the "rights of the people" were being "filched from them." It began on March 24, 1906, when the owners of 30 factories announced the firing of anyone wishing to remain in the unions. Though roughly one-half of the town's plants were involved, none were closed, and owners claimed "the quitting of the Union men will amount to nothing." After three weeks of claims and counter-claims, enough workers returned to their jobs to declare the situation closed. Farriss reported in 1906 that the town had solved its labor problem "in its own way."

Having survived a recession in 1904, and the labor problem "solved," High Point's businessmen returned to the notion that the city needed its own furniture show. Formed by Ralph Parker and "about half a dozen" manufacturers, the High Point Exposition Company had opened for its first show on January 1, 1905. Promoted as open "at all times," the exposition displayed 48 categories of home furnishings in 2,000 square feet on the second floor of the Maddox Building, at the corner of Broad and Elm Streets. The following year the Furniture Manufacturers Exhibition Company, managed by M. J. Freeman, had opened in 10,000 square feet on the third floor of the Ragan-Millis Building on South Main Street. Among the more than 20 manufacturers participating in this endeavor were Globe Home Furniture, High Point Furniture, Eagle Furniture,

Dalton Furniture, and Southern Furniture.

Showrooms such as these, however, did not attract attention like the annual exhibits held in the northern cities. So three years later, High Point Exposition Company was reorganized as High Point Associated Furniture Lines and joined with Furniture Manufacturers Exhibition Company to create a new and larger High Point Exposition Company. Two key figures in this development were W. G. Bradshaw, a physician active in several furniture firms, and Charles F. Tomlinson, secretary-treasurer of Tomlinson Chair Manufacturing. In an attempt to attract national buyers, they planned to hold two regularly scheduled expositions each year in January and June.

The first show was held March 1-15, 1909. According to a promotional flier "40 great factories" exhibited products in "five spacious showrooms," including Alma Furniture (kitchen furniture), Dalton Furniture (chamber suites), Globe Parlor Furniture (uphol-stered furniture), Continental Furniture (high-grade chamber suites), and Tomlinson Chair Manufacturing (dining suites, bedroom suites, living room suites, chairs, and rockers). Signed by Stephen C. Clark, secretary of the High Point Market Association, the handbill touted the city as the "one furniture district that holds out any hope to the dealer" and quoted a "New York buyer" as saying "I am delighted with the quality and variety of goods shown here and tickled to death with the prices." A second showing was scheduled for June 15-July 15 that summer. The results of both were disappointing. Buyers came, but mostly from the South. No third show was planned. Instead, in the years before the First World War, expositions continued, but were usually small in scope and aggressively competitive

J.W. Harriss, president, Harriss & Covington Hosiery Mills.
Photo courtesy The High Point Museum Archives.

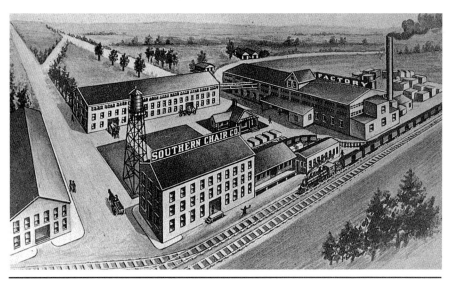

Southern Chair Company. *Photo courtesy The High Point Museum Archives.*

for those buyers who did attend. Five exposition companies were active in High Point in 1912, but the vision of one major exposition in a single building remained clear.

On March 8, 1913, the Southern Furniture Exposition Company was formed, with Charles F. Tomlinson as president. By concentrating exhibits in eight buildings twice a year in midsummer and midwinter, the first show, scheduled to open June 26, was expected to reverse the trend of mediocrity. With 100 exhibitors, the exposition eventually attracted 300 buyers during its three weeks. The following January the exposition resulted in similarly disappointing attendance. Undeterred, a third show was held in July 1914, but when hostilities broke out in Europe that summer, hopes faded once again. It would not be until after the First World War that the effort for a regular exposition would be renewed.

Though the United States would not become directly involved in the war for three years, High Pointers began feeling the effects of it immediately as the demand for durable goods disappeared with the interruption of farm exports. In only two months, factories were forced to drop production by half. Concerned that workers would be forced to leave town to find jobs, the city council

agreed to put men to work chopping wood for the needy. Citing past difficulties in obtaining manpower, the *Southern Furniture Journal* warned that "every laborer in High Point should be given all the employment possible." But the following year, the Allies opened war trade that brought a boom greater than the bust of 1914. Shortages in both labor and raw materials developed, but the *Journal* still happily proclaimed a return to "the good old days."

By the end of the Great War another industrial presence was being felt in the Furniture City. There were nine textile operations in the town in 1915, including five hosiery and two cotton mills. Two years of European war demand nearly doubled that figure, adding five more hosiery firms and three underwear companies. Small "mill villages" were now growing around Pickett Cotton Mill and Highland Cotton Mill. Adams and Millis had been joined in the hosiery business by mills with names like Crown, Royal, Amos, and Slane.

On April 18, 1919, five months after the end of the war, the Southern Furniture Exposition Company heard a report from Charles F. Long, a salesman and a manufacturer of mirrors, on a recent visit to an eight-story exposition building in Jamestown, New York. Determined once again to make regular exhibitions in High Point a reality, a committee was appointed to raise funds and to select a site for a similar building. Ten thousand dollars was raised in two weeks, and by June 5, a lot was acquired on South Main Street, two blocks south of the railroad. The $35,000 purchase was, according to the *Enterprise*, "one of the most important real estate deals in the history of the city." The company was renamed the Southern Furniture Exposition Building, Inc., with Charles F. Tomlinson as president, A. E. Tate as vice president, R. B. Terry as second vice president, and Charles Long as secretary-treasurer and manager. Other charter board members were B. F. Huntley, J. W. Harris, Fred N. Tate, M. J. Wrenn, A. S. Parker, S. L. Davis, F. S. Lambeth, R. R. Ragan, Frank Wineski, F. G. Hogland, and J. Elwood Cox. Contracts were awarded and ground was broken in August for construction of the 10-story building, at a cost of $1 million.

When the Southern Furniture Exposition Building opened for the first time to furniture buyers on Monday, June 20, 1921, the products of 149 manufacturers were displayed in its 249,000 square feet of showroom space. By noontime, 280 buyers registered for admission. During the first week they placed over $1 million in orders. By its conclusion on July 2, manufacturers had received another $2 million in orders from the 700 buyers who attended that first market in the new building. Buyers were accommodated through housing arrangements in High Point, Greensboro, and Winston-Salem. They were treated to "dutch" luncheons and entertained at welcome events planned by Harry Raymond, a distributor of veneers to manufacturers. Subsequent events achieved widening success. Initially planned for every three months, the schedule was curtailed to semi-annual showings in summer and winter after the July 1922 exhibit.

By 1924 every foot of the building's exhibit space had been rented and a waiting list started. High Point, which had become a center of furniture manufacturing, was now a marketing center as well. ∞

Southern Furniture Exposition Building. *Reprinted with permission of the Curt Teich Postcard Archives/Lake County (IL) Museum.*

Aldermen of High Point, circa 1895. *Front row, left to right:* A.R. Hammer, W.H. Ragan, Capt. William H. Snow (mayor), John A. Lindsay, E.A. Snow. *Back row, left to right:* J.P. Redding, D.C. Aldridge, Z.A. Burns, J.C. Welch. *Photo courtesy The High Point Museum Archives.*

North State Telephone linemen on Main Street in front of the Elwood Hotel.
Photo courtesy The High Point Museum Archives.

Perley A. Thomas took over the failing Southern Car Company (founded 1903) in 1916 and renamed it the P. A. Thomas Car Works. It later became the Thomas Built Bus Company, one of the world's largest manufacturers of school buses and other specialized vehicles. *Photo courtesy The High Point Museum Archives.*

A.B. Horney, High Point's first fire chief.
Photo courtesy The High Point Museum Archives.

High Point's first fire truck, circa 1915. The truck lasted one month and was returned. *Photo courtesy The High Point Museum Archives.*

adopted a fire department ordinance in 1903, naming Horney as fire chief, and legally empowering the firefighters to act in times of crisis. The volunteers were excused from poll taxes, and the chief was relieved of all taxes, as well as water and power fees. Fire inspections were to be conducted annually by Lovelace. The original "Northside" and "Southside" units were based in converted houses, while a third, "West End" company, constructed a small building on land donated by Myrtle Furniture Company. Contracts for construction of an official Northside Fire Station and City Hall were awarded in June 1908. Within the next few years, Southside and West End Fire Stations were also opened.

High Point had maintained a police "force" from its inception; but, incredibly, until 1900, it was composed of only one officer. In 1903 J. J. Farriss reported, "It is astounding to strangers that two policemen are sufficient to preserve order." Their peacekeeping activities focused on stamping out gambling and enforcing the temperance laws, but the continuous growth of the population was making their job more difficult, and the size of the force steadily grew. Parts of the town such as Beamon Street, "Moon Town," and "Bencini Row" were gaining infamy. On September 13, 1913, the city was shocked to learn that patrolman James W. Witcher had been killed attempting to stop a fight outside a theater on Washington Street. By 1915 the department had grown to eight officers.

Though the populace had been supplying partial funds for a "public" subscription

High Point police force, circa 1910. *Photo courtesy The High Point Museum Archives.*

High Point Normal and Industrial Institute classroom building.
Photo courtesy The High Point Museum Archives.

the Institute in Asheboro shortly after the Civil War. The High Point Normal and Industrial Institute conducted its first classes in a two-room frame building, then, in 1893, moved to a site on Washington Street. The society turned the school's administration over to a new principal, Dr. Alfred J. Griffin, in 1897. By 1902 enrollment totaled 287, as students received instruction in trades as well as academics, and even constructed a three-story hall in 1900.

It was not until 1897 that High Point committed itself to a formal graded school system. Though having rejected a similar proposal two years before, voters approved $10,000 for school bonds that spring and elected a board of

Dr. Alfred J. Griffin, principal of High Point Normal and Industrial Institute.
Photo courtesy The High Point Museum Archives.

school since 1882, High Point still entered the 1890s without a public education system. Such subscription schools, private academies, and seminaries had supplied superficial instruction with limited resources, and were often short-lived. In 1889 the High Point Female College, formerly of Thomasville, moved into the old Female Normal School building at the corner of Broad and College Streets, which dated to before the Civil War. It survived through 1893. The following four years, the High Point Institute and Business College occupied the structure, enrolling 300 children a year.

Ironically, a school for black children which was added to the city in 1891 likely provided its most reliable instruction. The New York Society of Friends had established

commissioners headed by J. Elwood Cox. George H. Crowell, a native of Stanly County and a graduate of the University of North Carolina, was named superintendent. Fortunately, the board chairman's wife, Bertha Cox, had not found the imposing stone residence her husband had recently constructed to her liking. In September, the High Point Graded School opened in what was the J. Elwood Cox home at the corner of Green and Main Streets, with 9 grades, a faculty of 10 teachers, and an enrollment of 400 pupils. Over the next 15 years, schools were located in each of the four wards in the town. The Normal and Industrial Institute became a "separate" part of the city system in 1924 as William Penn High School. A new high school for white students, High Point (later

Faculty at Elm Street School, 1903. *Front row, left to right*: Professor Gregory Crowell, Eunice Worth, Clara Boyd, Lillie Sherrod, and Cannon Reid. *Second row, left to right*: Aurelia Lindsay, Emma Blair, Vera Idol, Carey Jones, and Emma King. *Back row, left to right*: Notre Johnson, Martha Blair, Miss Legrand, Pauline Egbert, and Lucille Armfield.
Photo courtesy The High Point Museum Archives.

Sixth "B" grade at Elm Street School, 1908. *Front row, left to right*: William London, Robert Crissom, Hal Ingram, James Hoover, Rodney Snow, Marsh White, Oscar Richardson, and John Peacock. *Second row, left to right*: Jessie Cecil, Juanita Homme, Helen Gardner, Margaret Brown, and Annabelle Willis. *Third row, left to right*: Vernon Sechrest, Fred Lambeth, Edna Sechrest, Viola Younts, Nina White, Aileen Pitts, Mary Denson, and Andrew Lindsay. *Back row, left to right*: Lillie Belle Teague, Iris Council, Ruth Sechrest, Pauline Pugh, and Miss Ada Blair.
Photo courtesy The High Point Museum Archives.

High Point Graded School, South Main Street, circa 1910. This building was used from 1897 to 1931.
Photo courtesy The High Point Museum Archives.

Aerial photo of High Point College (now University), 1924. *Left to right are*: McCulloch Hall, Roberts Hall, and Woman's Hall.
Photo courtesy The High Point Museum Archives.

Central) High School, opened in 1927.

Educational opportunities broadened further when the Methodist Protestant Church established a four-year liberal arts college in the town. The board of education of the North Carolina Conference of the church favored High Point over Greensboro and Burlington as the site for the new school in a decision made on May 2, 1921. A community-wide campaign was mounted, pledging 60 acres and $100,000. Six of 20 members of the first board of trustees were from the town. High Point College opened in September 1924 with three buildings— Roberts Hall, an administrative building; McCulloch Hall, a male dormitory; and Woman's Hall.

With the added cost and complexity of running an industrialized municipality came increased disagreement, and the previously calm nature of High Point politics also began to change. Partisan politics had been practically unknown since the Reconstruction period, but the village governmental framework was no longer able to

handle the day-to-day management of a city, so a new charter was framed and approved in 1908. Only seven years later, it, too, was replaced by the general assembly, this time with a "commission" format. Though happy with the creation of a full-time city manager's position, the populace lamented the elimination of the board of education. Even more, they resented the establishment of partisan elections so much that two years later the state rescinded this provision. The board of school commissioners was restored in 1919. Industrialists were withdrawing from active participation in the municipal government, so that by 1921 not one of the commission members was a factory owner.

More political upheaval whirled around the city's relationship with its "county" cousin, Greensboro. As the Furniture City continued to grow, its citizens looked forward to the day that their town would surpass the "Gate City" in size. Displeasure was often expressed at the county commissioners' spending of High Pointers' money. Secession was even proposed. In 1913 the town's state legislator, Thomas J.

Company "M" High Point Rifles, a National Guard unit that
served in World War I.
Photo courtesy The High Point Museum Archives.

Nannie Kilby, owner of Kilby Hotel from circa 1910
until her death in 1921, and prominent African-
American businesswoman. *Photo courtesy The High
Point Museum Archives.*

the Kaiser and his Huns. Too soon High Point's citizens were purchasing war bonds from the city's banks and registering over 1700 young men for the draft. By August 1917, 97 men had already been selected for service, and the first company of volunteers was on its way to France. Freight not marked for the war effort sat idly on loading docks. Factories converted production from furniture to airplane propellers and wagon parts, while textile makers produced apparel for the troops. June 1918 brought the town its first news of casualties, and the list of dead and wounded began to grow quickly.

Another enemy "as relentless as the Hun" was creeping toward High Point in the form of the most contagious and deadly influenza ever known. It had already caused significant deaths in Europe, including over eight million in Spain, thus taking the name "Spanish Flu." It arrived in September, and town leaders moved quickly, realizing the havoc of the illness in other communities. Public assemblies were banned, affecting theaters, clubs, amusements, and even churches; but, such closings did little good, as factories and businesses remained open. Symptoms included pain in the eyes, ears, head, and back, dizziness, vomiting, blisters, nosebleeds, coughing, oppressive fever, and delirium. By mid-October there were over 700 cases, and 15 had died, including the mayor, W. P. Ragan. Before it was over, these numbers would more than triple.

"GERMANY CAPITULATES" was the headline in the extra edition of the November 11 edition of the *Enterprise*. But a brutal irony was being borne out as soldiers returned home. Such was the story with Private Edward Bryant, who left High Point with the first group of soldiers, served through the entire war, was severely wounded near its end, and returned home in January 1919 to find that the flu had taken his mother and father, and one of his two sisters.

The return to prosperity was once again thwarted in August 1919, this time by the city's second major labor dispute. A labor

Gold, introduced the "Aycock County Bill," which called for the creation of a new county from portions of Guilford, Randolph, and Davidson Counties. High Point would be its seat, of course. Though rejected by the general assembly, the result of the "Greensboro lobby," the topic remained in the press for several years to come.

But the local political conflicts were overshadowed by the genuine fighting on the battlefields of Europe. Between the opening of World War I in 1914 and the United States' entry into the fray three years afterward, residents followed the efforts of the Allies against surplus resulted in lower wages across the country as the military returned thousands to the workforce. Owners recognized that union organization had begun to creep back into the factories, and tried to replicate the success of 1906 by dismissing six vocal members. A full-scale walkout ensued in protest, and this time the workers proved to be more resolved. They were threatening those who attempted to cross picket lines, and several that did were injured during the seven-week shutdown. In the end, the governor, Thomas Bickett, volunteered to mediate a settlement, which allowed workers to join unions, but eliminated the possibility of forced membership.

The 1920s can, in many ways, be viewed as High Point's "Golden Age." Once beyond the calamities of the previous decade, the city accelerated at a dizzying pace. With 26 textile plants in operation in 1926, the town proclaimed itself "The Hosiery Capital of the South." Besides the exposition building, two other 10-story structures were constructed during 1921—the Commercial National Bank and the Sheraton Hotel. Roads were paved, parks were established, and schools were constructed. To raise funds for a new city hall, the general assembly was asked to grant a new charter which added over 6,500 citizens through voluntary annexation. A census with the new boundaries in 1923 set High Point as the sixth largest municipality in the state, surpassing arch-rival Greensboro by 3,000. It had become the epitome of industrial cities throughout the nation.

But the blessing was also a curse. Class division was becoming more apparent, as evidenced by the 1919 strike, and like most towns, High Point was residentially segregated. A new "residential masterpiece," Emerywood, was both "highly restricted and carefully developed," and by 1935 grew to 300 acres. The working-class neighborhoods, on the other hand, were filled with "crackerboxes." The *Enterprise* felt pride in its announcement that a woman had been named acting city manager in 1927, but only six years before it had boasted of having one

of the "largest [Ku Klux] Klans in the entire country." *Motor World* magazine raised the town's ire when it noted statistics showing High Point second only to Chicago in auto thefts for 1921. It would be years before "Little Chicago" could shake its local reputation for crime. Unfortunately, even darker days loomed ahead.

The stock market crash in October 1929

To support the U.S., the Giant Furniture Company manufactured airplane propellers instead of furniture during World War I.
Photo courtesy The High Point Museum Archives.

signaled the beginning of a difficult decade, a time of success and failure. At first the effects of the Great Depression were not much felt, but by early 1931 unemployment was rising and tax payments were declining. This was not good news for a city whose many bond-funded expansion projects had raised its indebtedness to more than $11 million. City Manager E. M. Knox saw the writing on the wall and declared in March that there would be no new spending; the debt must first be retired. Unfortunately, on July 31 he was forced to accept an additional $100,000 note from Commercial National Bank to avoid a foreclosure. The following January, this bank itself was out of business. City employees and policemen were laid off, while at the same time the numerous unemployed of the town

Reflections of the Past

were given odd jobs, including painting city hall. Throughout 1932, the citizens worked to raise money for the city, to avoid its default, but January 1933 found High Point out of money. A "Debt Plan" was drawn up, and the municipal government began the climb back toward solvency.

Although work was better in the local factories than in most others across the nation, and each year's furniture market expositions brought success, many in the town were without jobs. Beginning in 1933, the federal government began supplying funds to hire the unemployed for work on city projects. Wage-earners saw their pay being cut, often in half, and the local companies struggled to sell their products. Housing starts dropped to their lowest point in the century. In reaction, major strikes occurred in 1932, 1933, and 1934, each with considerable ill will and violence. Even the "Unemployment League," the public works employees, joined in the strikes.

Federal relief gave High Point amenities which its citizens could not afford. By February 1933 there were 12 distinct projects ongoing, including the building of water and sewer stations, fire department maintenance, street grading, and the construction of a gymnasium at High Point College and a new post office on Main Street. The most visible, however, were several major park developments. A new "city lake" for High Point had opened on Deep River with city funds in June 1931, and, during the same month, the David H. Blair family donated 73 acres on the town's southern boundary for a nine-hole golf course and tennis courts. Blair Park opened the following year, and expansions there continued. A major park was also being built on the banks of the city's reservoir, including an AAU specification pool which accommodated swimmers in the summer of 1935.

Though the town had a practically new water source, it was still having to purchase electricity from the Duke Power Company to sell to its residents through the city-owned lines. The rate negotiations with their supplier were a constant thorn in the city leaders' sides, so with the usual forward-looking optimism, they determined that they could assemble the funds necessary to construct a power dam on the Yadkin River that would produce enough cheap energy to light up High Point indefinitely. They did not count on a tenacious opposition from the power firm. From late 1936 to the end of the decade, a constant legal struggle ensued, but a confident Mayor C. S. Grayson felled the first tree in December 1938. The council was already receiving federal funds, and even awarded contracts for the project in April 1939. But litigation deterred full commitment, and little progress was made.

The Depression project which left the greatest mark was a joint effort of High Point, the North Carolina Highway Commission, Southern Railway, and the federal government. A railroad through the heart of the city had always been a source of death and delay, but as the population and automobile traffic grew, fatalities became commonplace. Civic leaders had been prodding the railroad executives for a solution for nearly 20 years. Initially conceived as a series of bridges over the rails, the idea appeared in 1925 for "a big ditch," a lowering of the tracks which would be significantly safer, and significantly more expensive. The railway was able to put off action until government funds finally brought it to feasibility, and an agreement was reached in December 1935.

Construction began on July 3, 1937. One month later, a timber bridge was opened at the Main Street intersection to permit crossing. Heavy rains brought numerous landslides which resulted in the deaths of several workers and the instability of buildings too close to the excavation. The first train passed through on March 29 of the following year. The "original" project was completed in September 1939, but depot renovations and the addition of supports and bridges continued for several years. The endeavor was not "completed" until 1947.

As the national economy began to pull

Southern Railway Depot and Main Street crossing before lowering of the tracks.
Photo courtesy The High Point Museum Archives.

Lowering of the railroad tracks. *Photo courtesy The High Point Museum Archives.*

out of the doldrums, the furniture industry was leading the trend. The *Enterprise* lamented that during the early 1930s there was "considerable empty space" during the markets. But, by mid-decade the building was once again filled, and in 1936 the Southern Furniture Exposition celebrated its 15th anniversary with record attendance and sales. An industrial assessment that year indicated that the total number of firms had increased nearly 20 percent since 1931, the largest gains in hardware suppliers and hosiery plants. Depression was turning to recovery in all of the city's businesses.

After four decades of innovation, growth, and expansion, High Point was fundamentally shaped as it would remain. Its bid to become the principal city in Guilford County had failed, and the municpality's financial footing had been shaken, but it had survived the tests of hardship and success, and was once again poised for the future. ∽

North Carolina's largest outdoor swimming pool at High Point's City Lake Park, circa 1940s.
Photo courtesy The High Point Museum Archives.

Downtown High Point, facing north from the Main Street bridge, circa 1939. *Photo courtesy The High Point Museum Archives.*

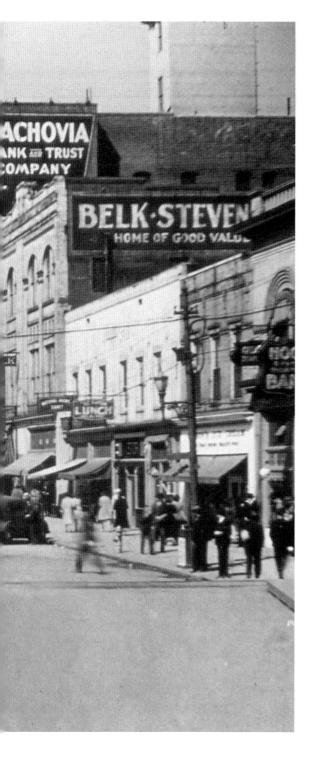

Chapter Four
A Familiar Image

A 1939 tourism guide to North Carolina, which was sponsored by the federal Work Projects Administration, described the Furniture City in very familiar terms. With the rails lowered, a bustling downtown, and large-scale furniture production—swimming, tennis, golf, movie theaters, markets and conventions—High Point now had the profile of a modern industrial city.

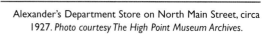

Alexander's Department Store on North Main Street, circa 1927. *Photo courtesy The High Point Museum Archives.*

Prosperity was back. The city's industries had recovered from economic distress, as evidenced by the announcement that a four-story addition planned for the top of the Southern Furniture Exposition Building had already been rented for the first five years by 40 new exhibitors. On Saturday afternoons the downtown streets took on a "carnival appearance" and sidewalks were "jammed with pedestrian traffic." But dark clouds loomed which threatened to spoil the optimistic outlook. As they had done before World War I, Americans watched the conflicts in Europe and the Pacific closely, anticipating the inevitable.

Clara Cox (1879-1940) was pastor of Springfield Friends Church for 21 years and was active in civic organizations that served women, children, and those in need. The Clara Cox Homes housing project was named in her honor in 1942.
Photo courtesy The High Point Museum Archives.

Beginning in 1940, the town pressed to upgrade the standard of living for many of its citizens by organizing a "Housing Authority." Though opposed as extravagant, it weathered claims that it demanded "luxurious conveniences" beyond those found in the average taxpayer's home, and with the aid of federal grants, began working on two major projects. Over 35 acres of "squalor born of poverty, tumble-down shacks," and "near-primitive 'sanitary' facilities" were cleared at two separate sites. Clara Cox Homes, the "white project," was named for the humanitarian daughter of business leader J. Elwood Cox. The Daniel Brooks Homes were for "the city's Negro population," and took their designation from an influential, turn-of-the-century black minister. The 450 "semi-apartment" units were occupied as they were completed throughout 1942.

While it sought to clean up deteriorating neighborhoods, High Point also found the need to purge its police force. The department had acquired a tarnished reputation during the previous decade through numerous accusations of selective enforcement and brutality, particularly toward the city's minority race, and internal investigations were viewed with great skepticism. The May 1933 legalization of beer sales had, for the first time, allowed citizens to lawfully consume alcohol, but illegal liquor continued to attract popular attention. Eight years later, several officers found themselves accused of colluding with bootleggers and gamblers, leading to several demotions and firings. The police force continued to struggle with its reputation; but, episodes such as three policemen "appropriating" confiscated beer for their own use, and charges of "extreme brutality" by arresting officers did not instill confidence in the citizenry.

The late summer of 1941 brought large numbers of visitors to town. In mid-August the AAU Women's National Swim Meet was held at the City Lake Park Complex. The competition drew national press coverage and spectators from across the country. Then for the following two months, thousands of

Reverend Daniel Brooks (1843-1933) was a Methodist minister in High Point from the 1870s to 1909. He helped negotiate the sale of land for the High Point Normal and Industrial Institute and promoted education in many ways. The Daniel Brooks Homes housing project was named in his honor in 1942. *Photo courtesy of Mrs. Gwen Davis.*

Carl Chavis, graduate of William Penn High School, gave his life in service to his country in France during World War II. He died while creating a smoke screen so his unit could cross the Moselle River. The Carl Chavis YMCA on Washington Drive is named in his honor.
Photo courtesy The High Point Museum Archives.

soldiers who had been engaged in war games in the Uwharries sought weekend entertainment and lodging. Dances, movies, auto races, free golf, and, of course, church services were offered for their diversion. Unfortunately, this only presaged what would soon become the ordinary in many other towns. Anticipating the coming struggle, the city governors had already announced both gas rationing, and a "Defense Council" to coordinate such efforts. Less than a month after the troops left the area, the *Enterprise* ran the extra edition which everyone had dreaded—"Japanese Attack Honolulu."

Efforts immediately commenced to prepare the town for war. With visions of the German bombing of London in their minds, an air-raid warning service was established using factory whistles, and citizens were reminded that industrial centers were common targets. Notice was to be taken of all "suspicious looking people." The Defense Committee described a turnout of 700 volunteers for work in the local "Civilian Defense" office as "pitiful." By New Year's Day, 1942, a rationing board had been named and a list of restricted items started. "Vital points" were guarded at night by "heavily-armed civilians." An emptiness was felt as

Centennial Parade, 1951, with Centennial Queen Mary Lou Culler sitting on an oversized chair by Tomlinson of High Point.
Photo courtesy The High Point Museum Archives.

High Point City Council, 1949-51. *Front row, left to right:* V.L. Hunt, Mayor William F. Bailey, C.A. Lewis, and R.B. Culler Sr. *Back row, left to right:* John W. Clinard Jr., William M. Burris, Robert Myers, Robert B. Rankin, J. Herman Teague, and Jesse H. Washburn. *Photo courtesy The High Point Museum Archives.*

housing vacancies were created by families leaving for defense jobs or military service, while factory production shifted to war-effort resources. Even so, City Manager E. M. Knox announced "definite, sweeping plans for long-range post-war municipal building," noting the necessity of getting in "on the ground floor" as government monies became available.

It was summer before the initial paranoia evolved into mediocrity as the fear of enemy bombs was replaced with the reality and hardship of the war's homefront. Shortage was the rule, not the exception, with everything primarily committed to defeating the Axis powers. Lumber was dedicated to crating supplies for the military, not domestic furniture. Hosiery production was limited to socks for the soldiers; so ladies' pre-war silk stockings became precious commodities.

Even labor was hard to come by for manufacturers of war goods trying to replace workers entering the armed services. Topping off the commitment of the city was the confiscation of the Southern Furniture Market Building in December 1942 by the Demobilized Personnel Records Branch of the Adjutant General's Office of the United States Army. For over four years there would be no furniture market.

Even so, the sacrifices of World War II were to pay big dividends for High Point. Not only did the Allies achieve the goal of eliminating Hitler and stopping Hirohito, but four years of pent-up demand coupled with unspent income meant plenty of consumers with plenty of money. As the GIs began returning in late 1945, factory owners moved quickly to resume their former means of production. Jobs were plentiful; housing was not. Price controls had to be maintained on staples to control inflation. Though the city and its denizens were ready to go to work, there was a problem—the army was not to relinquish its "lease" on the market building until May 1946, giving the other markets a year's jump on their southern competition. Indeed, it would be January 1947 before the momentous return of the buyers and exhibitors to the Southern Exposition.

Once the town got back to work, success compounded as businesses, old and new, raced to keep up with the tremendous demand. With over 5,000 buyers in attendance, more than double the pre-war levels, the first post-war High Point exhibition far exceeded expectations. During the war, government statistics revealed that North Carolina had surpassed New York as the leading furniture-producing state. The Southern Furniture Exposition Company had purchased the lot on the north side of the existing structure in 1944 for a large expansion, but shortages in labor and material delayed the start of the project until the last October of the decade. Stressing "the time element was vital," the million-dollar, 10-story addition was completed in a little over eight months, just before the July 1950 market.

High Point was once again flying high. As the furniture merchants were leaving, hundreds were arriving for a reprise of the AAU Women's National Swim Meet. Once again, the town gained nationwide attention and impressed visitors with its hospitality. But just as before the Second World War, the optimism of prosperity was being tempered by an unfolding conflict. United States soldiers had been committed in the first week of July to repel an invasion of South Korea by its northern counterpart. By the first week of September, the city's National Guard unit had been ordered to Fort Bragg and active duty. War again threatened the enterprise of the nation.

After eight months of back and forth fighting, the Korean conflict settled into two years of virtual stalemate. In High Point, as

in the rest of the nation, Americans hoped that "all-out" war was avoidable. Markets saw what was termed "scare-buying" during 1951, resulting from experiences with shortages and rationing less than a decade before. But civic leaders determined to provide citizens a rousing distraction. Focusing on the importance of the North Carolina Railroad to its founding, a "Centennial Celebration" was planned to commemorate "Cap'n" Gregg's prophetic naming of the city. Special events were held each day during the weeklong July celebration, and consummated after two rain-outs by a "pageant" of history held at the Albion-Millis Stadium at High Point College.

The signing of an armistice in Korea in July 1953 signaled a return of the momentum from the beginning of the decade. While

John Coltrane (1926-67), one of the world's most influential jazz musicians, lived in High Point until he was 17 years old. He attended Leonard Street Elementary and William Penn High School. *Photo courtesy The High Point Museum Archives.*

the country saluted returning soldiers and prisoners of war, High Point was welcoming furniture merchants to its first official "off-season" show in October which, curiously, attracted record crowds. Furniture heads had, for about 15 years, accommodated "in-between" buyers, principally northern sales-men who normally attended rival events in Chicago and Grand Rapids. Leaders had con-sidered the notion of formalizing additional shows as recently as 1948, but judged them unlikely for success. Southern manufacturers had assumed leadership in style and fashion after World War II, adding to the desire of retailers from beyond southern boundaries to tour the High Point exhibits. This surprising attendance confirmed a four-event-per-year rotation.

The municipal government had made a full recovery from its fiscal woes of the 1930s, and was recognizing it was not des-tined to be the largest city in the state, or even in the county. Reality dictated that High Point did not need its own airport, nor did it need a hydroelectric station on the Yadkin River, so both projects were dropped. The abattoir which had been operated for decades was leased to private interests. A large city park in the downtown was viewed as unnecessary, so Tate Park was sold, and "The World's Largest Bureau" moved to a new location. The community had pitched in with federal and state monies to construct a new hospital facility, which opened in December 1950. Plans were drawn for a new public library, and a combination city-county courthouse building. The library was com-pleted in 1953, but legal and financial impediments forced the other project into the next decade. New departmental equip-ment, such the addition of "a shiney new fire engine," became commonplace.

Those resources, especially those of the fire department, were sorely tested through the events of July 12, 1954. At 10:00 P.M. that evening, a fire was reported at the Jiffy Manufacturing Company, a carton-maker on West Green Street. All but one of the town's stations were summoned, and still it took two hours to control the blaze. As they were collect-ing the hoses, word came that the Tate Building, three blocks east beyond Main Street, was burning. Recognizing a potential catastro-phe, "urgent requests for assistance" went out to all fire units within a one hundred mile radius as the flames began to spread out of control. Before it could be contained, a third problem was discovered in the Snow Lumber-yard, a block back toward Main. The "boys from other towns" were credited with saving High Point, as everyone expressed doubt that the local department would have been enough to stop the holocaust. In the days following the conflagration, efforts were directed at finding the mysterious figure which Snow's night-watchman had chased from the lumberyard just before that fire was discovered.

In less than 10 years, the expansions of the late 1940s were proving themselves to be patches at best, for nearly everything in town was bursting at the seams. The year 1955 alone saw the construction of numerous industrial facilities, the initiation of a drive to enlarge the new hospital, the dedication of another addition to the Southern Furniture Exposition, and the announcement of a com-peting 12-story facility on the opposite side of Main Street. Success pushed the original exhibition building across Wrenn Street, liter-ally, when a seven-floor annex opened for the January 1959 market, straddling the thor-oughfare with an enclosed walkway from the third to the seventh floors.

After World War II, High Point faced problems of social development common to cities across the nation, particularly, the sig-nificant shift of certain population segments to the suburbs. This "trend for migration to the fringe area" forced consideration of annexation issues in late 1951, but the "over-whelming opposition" of those who were to be absorbed influenced city council members to "drop the idea." Progressive citizens began agitating for a liquor sales referendum, a common occurrence in southern cities in the 1950s, but lawmakers felt the impetus too weak for a vote. The council did, however, attempt to soften the "Blue Law" after a curb market operator was arrested, designating himself as a "test case." The public hue and cry convinced the leadership to rescind their revisions, returning to the original form of the ordinance. The "anonymous" liquor lobby did manage to bring that issue to public vote in 1955, but found resounding defeat by a more than two-to-one margin.

Without question, the crucial social issue the city faced in common with the whole nation centered on race. The town had often boasted through the years of its "excellent race relations," and exuded pride in its minority group's contributions of "honest labor and upright civic mindedness." In 1943 Arnold Koonce had promised two police officers of their own to the black community if he won the mayor's seat. Their 600 critical votes made High Point the first southern city with "Colored Patrolmen" when O. H. Leak and B. A. Steele were hired later that year.

The white population was generally unprepared for the dramatic changes in their society which began with the United States Supreme Court declaration in May 1954, that, when applied to educational facilities, separate could never be equal. It quickly became obvious that the same was true for every aspect of segregation, and the "colored people" of High Point began looking for opportunities to press for change.

The first steps in the march toward freedom were taken on the Blair Park Golf Course. On December 29, 1954, Dr. H. H. Creft, Dr. Perry Little, and another companion entered the clubhouse and asked permission to play. Though "there were no hard words," the attendant golf professional explained that he "had no authority to allow them to play." The same men had attempted to use the course about a month previous, but had been turned away. Placing the green fees on the counter, the trio enjoyed nine holes of golf that afternoon, and returned for a repeat performance two days later. When asked what the city council would do, Mayor

George Covington responded with no plan of action. "We were just waiting to see what they intended to do."

What they intended to do was find if the implications of the recent court decision would result in real change. Before a month had passed, the council had convened to hear the recommendation of their parks and recreation commission to "hold the line against integration." The councilmen, however, recognized the potential of "its toughest problem." Said one member, "They have given us a 'what' but no 'how.' I frankly don't at this time see a solution."

Suggestions ranged to the extreme of turning the facility over to private interests who could "legally" deny minority players, but city officials met with the "interested Negroes" and reached an understanding, though they failed to act for over a year. Finally, on March 1, 1956, Blair Park became the second "unsegregated" golf course in North Carolina.

It seemed there was reason for hope among the city's black population. The first step, though slow, had been painless. But local officials of the National Association for the Advancement of Colored People (NAACP) had already made it clear that more "immediate steps" were expected. In August 1955, petitions were handed to the school board calling for "steps to reorganize the public schools," noting the "time for delay, evasion and procrastination is past."

Despite NAACP pressure, school officials were able to forestall token integration until the summer of 1959. One week before school was to begin, the board "assigned" eleventh grader Lynn Fountain to the white Senior High School and her sister Brenda, a ninth grader, to the Ferndale Junior High. The two were selected apart from 15 others because they had previously attended racially "mixed" schools in New York City. Part of the announcement was a call for "support and prayers," and a statement declaring the "opinion" that "schools should not be used as a tool for espousing and bringing about integration."

O.H. Leak retired in September 1975 as captain of the Criminal Investigation Division. *Photo courtesy The High Point Museum Archives.*

B.A. Steele left the police force in August 1956 as a detective. *Photo courtesy The High Point Museum Archives.*

Lynn and Brenda Fountain leaving school administration building, accompanied by Dr. Perry Little and Reverend B. Elton Cox. *Photo courtesy The High Point Museum Archives.*

September 1, the first day of classes, was obviously tense, but the "milestone" was passed in what was described as "commendable fashion." During the night, unknown parties painted the message "Go Home Nigger" on the high school drive, but a group of students voluntarily removed it before the arrival of the new pupils. A few "unauthorized" vehicles prowled the area, but left without incident. Officials described the day as "completely normal," and the girls' mother expressed hope that "High Point has too many Christian people in it to let a few hoodlums take over." Unfortunately, the power of the racial question would prevent the fulfillment of her dream.

During the decade of the 1960s the Vietnam War, urban renewal, downtown development, and annexation battles repeatedly grabbed headlines. Liquor, blue laws, and morality ordinances continued to be debated, and a strong economy helped the town's industries, along with the Southern Furniture Market, maintain vigorous expansions. But without question, the racial struggle remained one of the most significant experiences of the time.

On February 1, 1960, four college students sat down at Woolworth's lunch counter in downtown Greensboro, igniting a fire of protest which would fan out across the South. Citizens of High Point watched their neighbors' struggle with cautious anticipation. As the days passed, similar protests appeared in other North Carolina towns like Durham, Raleigh, Charlotte, and Winston-Salem, each the home of a Negro college.

On the 11th of February, 26 students from William Penn High School took seats at the South Main Street Woolworth's lunch counter to start the movement's first non-college student protest; a week before, the young people had approached B. Elton Cox, pastor of the Pilgrim Congregational Church, asking for advice on how they might join the growing movement. Two civil-rights workers arrived, one from Durham and one from Birmingham, Alabama, to help organize the demonstration. Rumors had been spreading for days that a demonstration was planned, and a number of "young whites" quickly took up posts in the store as word circulated about the effort. The store manager closed the counter immediately, and the entire store 20 minutes later.

The following day, the protesters returned, and scuffles ensued at Woolworth's counter between young whites who had already secured all of the seats and the black youths who wanted them. The usual weekend shutdowns coupled with a 10-inch snowfall brought calm to the city for the weekend, but it was not to last. On February 14, a group of "50-odd young whites" hurled snowballs, striking both their intended victims and bystanders.

The fears of many were brought to fruition the next day, February 15. Representatives from the Chamber of

Protesters marching on Main Street in 1963. *Photo courtesy The High Point Museum Archives.*

Commerce and the Merchants Association met with a group of "five self-styled leaders of the white opposition" to convince them that "gang warfare is no good," but to no avail. Late in the afternoon, a large group of protesters marched into the downtown area. A 10-minute "flurry of rock and bottle throwing" erupted at the intersection of Hamilton and Washington. The clash was the first major violence associated with the burgeoning sit-in efforts.

Strong community reaction led to negotiation and a truce. Mayor Jesse Washburn appointed an "Inter-racial Committee" to "bring peace to High Point," and attempt to settle the lunch counter question. Protests

were suspended and the dining areas remained closed. Eventually, agreement was reached and no further protests occurred.

After the initial conflict, the dissidents were managed through the efforts of the Congress of Racial Equality (CORE). The national civil rights organization had been impressed with the local efforts, and in June 1961 placed B. Elton Cox on its payroll as a "field secretary." Their goal was to create an "open city," and their policy was one of peaceful, disciplined demonstrations. The struggle continued on a smaller scale for the next few years, and often concentrated on two downtown movie theaters which still forced minority residents to purchase tickets at side

Capus Waynick. *Photo courtesy The High Point Museum Archives.*

entrances and sit only in the balcony. The school assignment process was also a common target for protest. By 1963 the white leadership boasted of advances such as integrated tennis courts, swimming pools, and the naming of members to the parks commission, school board, and ministerial alliance. In late February it was announced that High Point had been named an "All-America City" in part because of its "progress in race relations." This perspective was viewed with impatience by the black community.

Spring of 1963 brought an increase in the protest efforts. A "mass meeting" was scheduled for May 24 with James Farmer, the national director of CORE, as the scheduled speaker. For the next five nights marchers paraded from the Washington Street neighborhood through the downtown area, always jeered and harassed by "a larger crowd of whites, most of them young boys." On the fifth night, smoke bombs and rocks were tossed at the protesters, once again leading to panicked negotiations which resulted in a two-week truce, and the formation of a "Biracial Committee" charged with expediting the integration process.

The new committee was headed by High Point native Capus Waynick, who had returned to the city to begin his retirement only one day before the mass marches began. Waynick, a former *Enterprise* editor, had served as a United States Ambassador to both Nicaragua and Columbia, and in various other state and federal posts. But the progress of the Biracial Committee proved too slow, and by the first of September, full scale marches were revived. For 10 days protesters filed two-by-two through the heart of town as whites lined the sidewalks, some to watch, some to taunt. Each night brought increased tension and a growing number of arrests, over 300 on the evening of September 9. Protest leaders threatened various disruptions during the upcoming furniture market. The situation was becoming "grave."

On September 12 councilmen pondered ordinances which would restrict picketing and "parades." Mayor Floyd Mehan and Reverend B. Elton Cox organized a meeting between the opposing leaders during the afternoon. An agreement was reached with three principal items. First, mass demonstrations would be "called off." Secondly, the city council would scrap the contemplated protest laws. Thirdly, the city would create a permanent "Human Relations Commission," which would replace the temporary "Biracial Committee." December 6 was set by the antisegregation leadership as an evaluation "deadline." If significant progress was not made, protests would then be resumed.

Representatives from the local chapters of both CORE and the NAACP announced their satisfaction with the work of the commission. Some downtown businessmen were still denying service to blacks, but the inevitability of change was now obvious. While never relenting on the rights which they felt were theirs, the desegregation leadership had, during the course of the movement, acknowledged several times that High Point was in the forefront of "openness" among North Carolina cities. Though the struggles continued, particularly in the area of "real" school integration, mass protest was never again applied.

The challenges which High Point faced between World War II and the early 1970s were similar to those faced by communities across the South. Maturity came with the answering of each challenge. It no longer seemed necessary to strive to be the largest in Guilford County, as a higher quality of life for all its citizens became the focus. The city began to find its place in the world, and the world now recognized High Point as its furniture marketing capital.

The Southern Furniture Market had continued to expand throughout the 1960s, both in attendance and floor space. In 1973 the city government was left without a home as the Southern Furniture Market Center acquired city hall and the city-owned Paramount Theatre for the erection of its Commerce Street Wing. While the new showroom addition included a modern theatre facility for the community, it was two years before the scattered offices were recollected into the new city hall. Despite a deepening recession which hurt High Point's textile and hosiery industries particularly, the furniture markets remained strong. Competition loomed, however, in the form of regional exhibitions in Dallas and Atlanta. The rising apprehension among furniture leadership led some of them to Dallas in January 1976, to observe, first-hand, the upstart show. They reported a more festive atmosphere where salesmen and buyers alike could combine business and pleasure.

Furniture executives and city leaders remembered that High Point had successfully "stolen" the national marketing show from places like Chicago, Grand Rapids, and Jamestown, New York. They did not intend to have history repeat itself to the city's detriment. Although attendance and occupancy continued to reach all-time highs, warnings were issued about this possible threat. By mid-year, the community was moving to solidify its hold. Investors announced the renovation of the old Tomlinson Furniture Factory into a showplace facility of a half-million square feet, Market Square. A "market retention" committee was formed with two councilmen, two business representatives, and two members of the Chamber of Commerce. Chaired by Councilman Joe Patterson, its goal was to bring more convenience to the events through parking plans, hospitality centers, and increased housing assistance. Coincidentally, a liquor referendum was also placed on the coming November ballot by the city council. By the year's end confidence had been restored, and the threat put to rest. High Pointers had also voted to allow the opening of liquor stores after a vigorous campaign from both sides of the issue.

The following year, the city struck cultural gold with the founding of the North Carolina Shakespeare Festival; performances were in the new High Point Theatre constructed as part of the Commerce Street

Furniture Market buyers. *Photo courtesy of High Point Convention and Visitors Bureau.*

Wing. A metropolitan "feel" had been growing since the mid-1960s through organizations such as the High Point Arts Council and the High Point Historical Society, and continuing in the 1970s with the Piedmont Environmental Center. By the mid-1980s a myriad of guilds, associations, and foundations were giving area residents vast opportunities for entertainment, education, and participation. This, in concert with a strong economic base and employment potential, made the area very attractive for immigration; several national quality-of-life surveys placed High Point at or near the top.

Furniture factories had given High Point

New City Hall, 1975. *Photo courtesy The High Point Museum Archives.*

manufacturing roots, in turn giving rise to other major industries, such as hosiery and textiles. The furniture market had given the city a second economic strength, and helped property maintain a high value when other downtowns were failing. Ironically, diversity has been the city's chief characteristic in recent years. It is the home of leading manufacturers of buses and yachts, major photography studios, and even a movie soundstage. In 1983 the Chamber of Commerce launched a Convention and Visitors Bureau. Since that time, hundreds of conventions have made use of the tremendous resources available between furniture markets, resulting in millions of additional revenue dollars each year.

The leaders of the original village had struggled for a way to bring both immigrants and industry to High Point, but now their continuing success leaves citizens wondering how to cope with growth. Today's battles include questions about shopping malls, annexation, and highway routes. William Welch had promised buyers in 1853 that the land around the rail crossing was "healthful and promises fair to become one of the most thriving towns on the entire line of railroad." The challenge now remains to guarantee that his prophecy endures. ∞

Piedmont Centre, opened in 1988, has over 3.2 million square feet of office, manufacturing, and distribution space. It is home to more than 60 companies employing over 6,000 workers. *Photo courtesy of the City's Economic Development Corporation.*

Chapter Five

The Forward Reflection

 D. L. Clark had wondered at "living in a grown up city" in 1899. How would he feel about his beloved town a century later? What image does the mirror of history leave for High Point?

The Ferd Ecker Glass Company produced mirrors, such as this acid-etched one, in the early twentieth century, and was just one company that supplied component products to the furniture industry.
Photo courtesy The High Point Museum Archives.

The crossroads which created the city also attracted resourceful, imaginative people. It was a business town by birth, and the choice of its early citizens to make it an industrial center was natural. Persistence coupled with success produced what has been referred to as both the "High Point Spirit" and the "Spirit of Enterprise." This created a snowball effect, bringing others of superb business skills, building success upon success. Perseverance was a marked characteristic of the town's developers, as evidenced by the incessant endeavors to make it a marketing center before the breakthrough in 1921. The city's place in the world of manufacturing and marketing can be directly attributed to these qualities, and to the prowess of those who exhibited them.

In many ways, creating High Point was easier than maintaining it. The Great Depression, World War II, and the social struggles of the decades which followed produced "big city" problems for a population that was still somewhat "rural" in outlook. But once again, perseverance and focus were major factors in resolving these issues and conflicts, and in keeping the town prosperous. The opportunity now remains to continue this heritage.

The progressive nature of business in High Point and the increasing demand for furniture exhibition space combined to create a "vital" central business district. The "death of downtown" which posed such a great concern for urban renewal in the 1960s and 1970s faded as the city emerged as the premier international showplace for home furnishings during the 1980s, officially taking the designation "International Home Furnishings Market" in October 1989.

Consequently, the High Point of today bears no resemblance to the little city struggling to make a name for itself at the beginning of the twentieth century. As the century turns, can the heritage which made High Point a unique center of commerce be preserved without jeopardizing prosperity? Once again, the community must rely upon the resourceful and imaginative leadership similar to that which turned a simple intersection into the envy of many towns. The echoes still ring from the 1923 "Pageant of Progress," which was held to celebrate the halcyon days. To those citizens, it was obvious why their city had prospered. Its history was reflected in "The Spirit of Progress, Attended by Religion, Education, Industry, Art, Good Roads, Peace, Joy, Thanksgiving." ∞

Judy Mendenhall, High Point's first female mayor, was elected in 1985. She is credited with initiating increased economic development and investment such as Piedmont Centre business park. *Photo courtesy of* High Point Enterprise.

Bob Brown, pictured here with South African President Nelson Mandela (left), is founder of B & C Associates, Inc., a public relations firm with clients around the world. He also has served as special assistant on minority affairs to President Nixon, 1969-72. *Photo courtesy of Bob Brown.*

The Depot as viewed from the Main Street bridge, the highest point in High Point. *Photo courtesy The High Point Museum Archives.*

Alison Shanks and Mark Kincaid in the North Carolina Shakespeare Festival's production of *MacBeth*, 1995.
Photo by Koch Studio, Inc., courtesy of North Carolina Shakespeare Festival.

Visitors to High Point's City Lake Park may enjoy boating, fishing, picnicking, using the amusement rides, working out in the gymnasium, swimming in North Carolina's largest outdoor pool, or just watching a glorious sunset. *Photo courtesy of Piedmont Environmental Center.*

Reflections of the Past

Piedmont Environmental Center, constructed from recycled materials, is located on a 376-acre animal and plant preserve with over 11 miles of trails. *Photo courtesy of the Piedmont Environmental Center.*

Over 75,000 people from around the world attend the International Home Furnishings Market twice each year. "Markets" are held in April and October, and are only open to furniture retailers and interior decorators. Market is the largest single annual event in North Carolina, and brings in over $240 million into the regional economy.
Photo courtesy of High Point Convention and Visitors Bureau.

Oak Hollow Mall, with 950,000 square feet of retail space, opened in August 1995 after years of planning. *Photo courtesy of Oak Hollow Mall.*

High Point native General Maxwell Thurman, United States Army, rose to the rank of four-star general without attending West Point, one of few men to do so. He commanded the invasion of Panama and overthrow of General Manuel Noriega in 1989, and created the Army's slogan, "Be All You Can Be." *Photo courtesy The High Point Museum Archives.*

Sammie Chess was the first African-American Superior Court judge appointed in the South in the twentieth century.
Photo courtesy The High Point Museum Archives.

Siceloff Hardware Company on the 100 block of South Main Street, circa 1920s. *Left to right, behind counters:* John Siceloff, Arnold Craver, Charlie Miller (customers are unidentified). *Photo courtesy The High Point Museum Archives.*

Chapter Six
Partners in Progress

A group of prominent High Point businessmen, circa 1890. *Seated, left to right*: June J. Lindsay, W.P. Ragan, J. Elwood Cox, George A. Matton, J.D. Clinard, and R.G. (Bob) Cook. *Standing, left to right*: Ed L. Ragan, John R. Brown, Fred N. Tate, J.J. Farriss, R.G. Fortune, unidentified boy, Joe F. Hoffman, and Alec B. Smith. *Photo courtesy The High Point Museum Archives.*

Main Street looking north during the famous 1927 snowstorm. This storm is still remembered as one of the biggest weather events in High Point history. *Photo courtesy The High Point Museum Archives.*

Newell Beeson opened a hardware store at 216 North Main Street in 1883. Originally a business that sold buggies, harnesses, and farm equipment, Beeson's has since diversified its products and services to meet changing customer needs, but had remained a Main Street fixture for more than 100 years.

In 1896 Amos Ragan bought the store from Newell Beeson for $5,200. Ragan soon realized he needed help, so he summoned his son, Robert R. Ragan, home from Chapel Hill, where he was studying medicine. For 50 years, Beeson's owed its success and growth to Robert Ragan, who was president of the company from 1905 until his death in 1955.

By 1910 Beeson's occupied two four-story brick buildings on Main Street. Robert Ragan's early ventures into diversification included digging wells and installing pumps and septic tanks; building barns and tobacco flues and cures. Beeson Hardware was one of the first to actively pursue builders and contractors, as well as homeowners, and one of the first to carry building supplies. A lumber yard and woodworking shop were added in the 1920s, quickly followed by a roofing and sheet metal department. A finish hardware department, which furnished locks, hinges, doorknobs, and other accessories for homes, schools, stores, and hospitals was another thriving division.

During the Great Depression, Ragan lost almost everything, but quickly recovered and became a multimillionaire. During the 1930s, the store began carrying plumbing supplies, Frigidaire appliances, and Hoover vacuums. The growing furniture manufacturing industry also influenced the business; upholstery nails, sandpaper, casters, and dustdown were among the many items stocked for furniture production. Beeson's also carried sporting goods and had a Boy Scout department that flourished from the 1920s until the early 1980s.

Robert Ragan was a man of legendary frugality. He built his living quarters above the store and heated the rooms with a woodstove. His office was on the mezzanine overlooking the retail operations, and he kept a close eye on his employees. Many customers preferred to deal with him directly; and he would go through the warehouse areas personally to find the merchandise they wanted. When farmers didn't have cash, Ragan accepted payment in hay, grain, or cattle. When he made large cash sales, he stuck the money in his vest pocket and took it upstairs to the safe.

Ragan's business acumen is exemplified by the "horse collar incident." An employee forgot the name of a customer who purchased a collar. Ragan's solution was to bill every one of his customers for a horse collar. He found the missing customer—and sold an additional number of collars.

Uncle Bob had 13 nieces and nephews, and they inherited the business. Brooks Reitzel succeeded him as president. Reitzel served in that capacity for 20 years until his death in 1975. He was followed by Tom Robinson, who died a year later.

Ed Spivey has been president since 1976. Under his management, Beeson's moved from Main Street to Centennial, and expanded all its divisions. The store still prides itself on having a vast assortment of nuts and bolts, but the emphasis is now on industrial materials, builders' hardware, lumber, and the wholesale distribution of decorative hardware. The company that began as a little buggy shop in the early days of High Point now has more than 65 employees, and annual sales of more than $16 million. ∞

Established in 1883, Beeson Hardware & Lumber Company now serves its customers at the expanded North Centennial Street location.

Baptist Children's Homes of North Carolina, Inc.

One dark rainy Christmas Eve, Malinda's mother and her mother's boyfriend dumped her and a pitiful little suitcase at the end of a muddy dirt road to trudge to her grandmother's house. They didn't want her to live with them anymore.

Imagine Malinda standing in the rain, watching her mother drive away with a man she chose over her own child. Malinda turns and looks toward grandmother's house, a dark silhouette with a warm, glowing porch light beckoning her.

What if there had been no light?

Baptist Children's Homes of North Carolina (BCH) has been providing light for children like Malinda since 1885. Baptist minister John Mills founded BCH as the Thomasville Orphanage in an era when families were still disrupted from the Civil War. Mills had also founded the Oxford Orphanage in Oxford, North Carolina.

Baptist Children's Homes has since grown to serve more than 1,500 children each year through 12 facilities across North Carolina. Headquarters are located on the original Thomasville Orphanage campus, now known as Mills Home. Dr. Michael C. Blackwell has been BCH president since July 1, 1983.

BCH also operates residential campuses in Clyde, Pembroke, and Kinston; a maternity home in Asheville; Care House in Lenoir for teenage mothers and their babies; Noel Home in Lenoir and Moody Home in Franklin for girls who need behavior changes in problem solving; therapeutic camping at Cameron Boys Camp in Moore County, where 40 boys live year-round in shelters they build themselves; emergency care cottages on the campuses; and model day care in Thomasville.

Genese's mom would buy clothes for her children in the morning, and resell them for drugs that night. Genese never knew her father. When she came to BCH, she was determined not to love anyone. But staff "loved me no matter," and broke down her wall of darkness and pain.

Those BCH serves are not orphans anymore, but victims of abuse and neglect, most often from family members they love and trust. Many have been thrown out, ridiculed, addicted, and misused. Sometimes issues of rebellion surface, making it impossible even for loving parents to deal with their child themselves. Whatever the issues, BCH works with the child and with the family to restore the family unit whenever possible. If it becomes apparent that it is not possible, long-term care and post-high school education are offered.

It's not unusual for a child to follow the career path blazed by a parent. But when that career involves selling illegal substances, and its subsequent lawless lifestyle, it's a dead-end. When Stacey followed his mother's drug career, it led to stealing, fighting, and association with a bad group. "I didn't see any other way to go," Stacey said. BCH counselors made it clear he was headed for a hard time and a short life. Staff stuck with him as he worked through his anger. When Stacey left, he planned to earn a technical school degree, then pursue a career in law enforcement.

Baptist Children's Homes of North Carolina serves children and families across all lines of race, economic status, and religious affiliation. In 1996 its budget is $12.3 million, of which only one-fourth comes from Baptist churches. About 40 percent comes from payment for services. The rest is raised each year from friends who care about the next generation.

BCH shines bright lights of hope onto dark paths of despair for hurting children and broken families. ∞

Dozens of active North Carolina printers learned their trade by typesetting, printing, and mailing *Charity & Children*, the Baptist Children's Homes' weekly newspaper, as seen in this circa 1930 picture of the print shop. Today the paper is printed monthly and is distributed free of charge.

To help Baptist Children's Homes of North Carolina residents launch successful lives after experiencing traumatic setbacks, Piedmont Aviation Founder Thomas H. Davis (second from left) funded the Runway for Success at BCH. Children with leadership potential, like William, Clifton, and Ryanne participate in an inspirational seminar and take an educational trip. In 1994 the seminar was delivered by international businessman Nido Qubein, of High Point (fourth from left).

On every continent of the globe, soft drinks and beer are delivered in aluminum truck bodies built in High Point by the W. F. Mickey Body Company. These "rolling billboards" trace their lineage back to 1904, when young Will Franklin Mickey opened up a local blacksmith shop catering to area farmers who still preferred wagons over the then-fledgling automotive technology.

Carl Mickey Sr., the youngest of W. F. Mickey's four children, started working in his father's shop while he was still a schoolboy, learning his craft from a former slave known about town as "Uncle Jules." An ambitious student, young Mickey quickly learned the ins and outs of forging metal, rebuilding wagon wheels, and repairing farm tools.

The Mickey business, one of three blacksmith shops in town, changed addresses several times prior to World War II, but ever aware of the three most important rules in retail—location, location, location—W. F. never strayed beyond the friendly confines of "downtown," a very convenient venue for the farmers who ventured in for their weekly shopping trips.

The family business was exclusively "repair work" back then, recalls Carl Sr., who remembers sharpening lawnmowers, fixing farm equipment, and sharpening "about a million" digging tools for the likes of North State Telephone Company. Before long, the Mickeys had expanded their services to include modifying pick-up trucks for special uses. For his efforts, Carl Sr. earned three dollars a week, and his father threw in room and board.

While Carl Sr. was still in high school, working part-time and all through the summers, his father took ill, and the young Mickey was put in charge of the family business, admittedly a little prematurely. "I was in charge, but I didn't know how to price things," he remembers. "I called up another area businessman, and he said I should charge twice what the men who worked for us were being paid." He took the man's advice, even though it meant raising the

prices his father had established. "If they had been charging 15 cents to sharpen an ax, I asked for a quarter, or even 35 cents."

The war took Carl Mickey away from High Point, but not away from his passion for working with tools and "inventing better ways of making and fixing things." As a high school boy he had learned to fly, and during the war he served as an Air Force pilot, stationed in Lincoln, Nebraska. With a lot of time on his hands between flights, he found a

local blacksmith shop and worked there for nothing. While working with the elderly proprietor, Carl designed and built a trailer for one of his Air Force buddies. He may not have realized it then, but that trailer marked the birth of the modern-day Mickey Truck Bodies.

When he left the service, he returned to the family business and immediately struck a new deal with his father. "Papa would never borrow money, but I knew we would have to

Will Franklin Mickey, in his 30s

take a loan if we were going to grow the business," says Carl. "So I told him I'd pay him $50 a week and take care of all his hospital bills if he would let me have the business. He agreed to my terms and retired from the business. Now I could borrow money, and of course I immediately went into debt."

Sometimes, big ideas cost big money, and while he may have been short on capital, he certainly was not short on ideas. The first move Carl made was to build a much bigger shop, a 5,000- square-foot facility equipped with press brakes, air compressors, and everything that was needed to actually build a truck body. One of his first customers was National Bohemian, a brewery based in Baltimore. Word spread throughout the beer business, and before long, Mickey was specializing in building beer truck bodies.

Building these bodies came almost instinctively to Carl, who allows, "I never bought a truck body in my life. I just built what people wanted." His first bodies were made of wood. Then came wood and steel, then all steel, followed by steel and aluminum. Today the company designs and builds a wide line of all-aluminum bodies and trailers for several industries, including beverage, furniture, emergency services, home improvement, snack foods, and battery distribution. When Carl Sr. took over the company, an order for three trucks was a cause for celebration. Today it's not uncommon for Mickey to build up to 250 units for a single customer, and its customer portfolio reads like a Who's Who in American industry: Coca-Cola, Pepsi-Cola, Nabisco, Frito Lay, Heilig-Meyers, Lowe's, Anheuser-Busch, and Miller Beer, to name only a few. The company now

These 1950s-style Mickey truck bodies stand ready to deliver.

employs nearly 300 full-time employees—more than half with 10-year tenures—and operates four regional "reconditioning" facilities in New Jersey, Florida, Illinois, and North Carolina. Bodies and trailers are now designed on state-of-the-art CAD systems by Mickey's staff of professional engineers, and the products are built using sophisticated automated manufacturing equipment such as Amada punch presses. The company turns out about 4,000 units a year from its plant on Trinity Avenue, which has been expanded, renovated, and modernized no less than six or seven times over the years. And not only do the soft drink, beer, and furniture logos which Mickey craftsmen so meticulously apply to the sides of these bodies appear in the English language, but also in Russian, Arabic, and Spanish, among many others, based on their specific destinations. All told, Mickey bodies and trailers are sold in more than 20 countries around the world.

Dean Sink, Mickey president, believes that the company was really built on "Mr. Mickey's dissatisfaction." Although for years

Carl Mickey wore many hats—driving north to find customers, sleeping in his car, then returning to build products—he was always closest to the manufacturing process, and endlessly driven to improving both his manufacturing equipment, his production methods, and ultimately, his products.

Throughout it all, Carl Mickey never really paid much attention to the competition, mainly because he believed if he built a quality product, sold it at a fair price, and then stood behind it in case the customer wasn't completely satisfied—the three tenets of the modern-day Mickey—he knew his business would prosper. In fact, while other companies were closely guarding their manufacturing "secrets," Mickey felt perfectly comfortable turning competitors loose in his plant to pick up all the information they wanted. There was enough business to go around, he figured, and besides, he never wanted to be the biggest, just the best.

"I just wanted to build good products and have some fun along the way," he says today. Part of the fun, he adds, was designing and

This Budweiser truck was manufactured by the W. F. Mickey Body Co. in the late 1940s.

building some "strange animals"—like an innovative "Keg-O-Matic" beer truck equipped with a mechanism that allowed the keg to roll down an inside track and out a special door waist-high to the deliveryman. The idea was to save the driver the strain of having to bend over to lift the heavy kegs, or from having to reach up and pull one off the truck. It was a good idea at the time, but it fizzled out when the major breweries changed their keg sizes.

And after 92 years, the business is still owned and operated by the Mickey family, making it one of the oldest family-run companies in the United States. Dean Sink, Mr. Mickey's son-in-law, and Carl Mickey Jr., president and vice president, respectively, introduced Japanese management practices when they took over the reins in 1982. High productivity, just-in-time inventory, and absolute quality are the company's hallmarks, along with its innovative spirit and commitment to its employees.

As for Carl Sr., he still maintains an office at the plant, where a modern rowing machine takes its place among old "souvenirs" like the iron tool he made from a wagon wheel in the blacksmith shop of another era, and a Tuberose snuff tin that that belonged to his father. He's still experimenting with new and better ways of building truck bodies, and his curiosity is just as lively now as before. He likes to recall the past, but make no mistake; he is focused on the future. And oh, yes, he's still having fun. He wouldn't work for anything less. ∞

Mickey Truck Bodies' bodies and trailers are now designed on state-of-the-art CAD systems by Mickey's staff of professional engineers.

High Point Graded School graduating class of 1900. *Front row, left to right:* Sam Charles, Annie Tomlinson, Clara Kirkman, Helen Snow, Anna Kirkman and Vernon Idol. *Back row, left to right:* Ward Eshelman, Earl Carter, June Burton, Joe Cox, George Crowell (teacher), Virgil Idol, Jack Fields, Ed Millis and Charlie Ingram. *Photo courtesy The High Point Museum Archives.*

Junior Order Hospital, 1912

In 1904 an outbreak of typhoid fever established the need for a hospital in the young city of High Point. The Junior Order of American Mechanics responded by purchasing and remodeling a two-story frame house on Boulevard Street. That year, on a summer day, the hospital was inaugurated with an open house complete with lemonade and cookies. The furniture and bedding were donated, and the hospital staff of four nurses and a housekeeper was headed by Dr. John T. Burrus. The hospital had room for 12 patients, and a week's stay cost between $10 and $15.

Dr. Burrus and his associate, Dr. Guy Duncan, bought the hospital in 1912, and purchased adjacent land with an eye to expansion. In 1913 it was chartered as High Point Hospital, Inc. By then, the hospital had a five-year-old nursing school. Though not regulated by the state in its early years, the nursing school nonetheless turned out skilled and caring nurses. By the time it closed, in 1978, it had graduated 891 nurses in 70 years of operation. One of the earliest employees of the hospital was Andrew Corbett, who began working at the hospital in 1910. He stayed for 73 years, and when he

retired in his 90s, "Mr. Andrew" was the longest tenured hospital employee in the United States.

Dr. Burrus, who served the hospital until his death in 1935, was sorely missed when he served overseas during World War I. Surgery patients had to travel by train to Salisbury when he was gone. He returned from the war in 1919 with a new specialty—trauma care.

In the early part of the century, the hospital grew a room at a time, as each year's cash balance was turned over to improvements and expansions. During the 1920s, an X-ray machine and an emergency room were added. Also in that decade, the medical staff grew to include a Navy surgeon who established a diagnostic laboratory at the hospital, an ear, nose, and throat specialist, and a general surgeon. The hospital was equipped with a modern operating suite.

The Depression put an end to growth for several years. In 1929 hospital income was at the lowest point in its history. Nurses worked for food and lodging, but no salaries. The ear, nose, and throat specialist helped keep the hospital open by sending his tonsillectomy patients there instead of doing the surgeries in his office.

In 1933, after serving a term in the State Senate, Dr. Burrus decided to transfer ownership of the hospital to a nonprofit corporation to ensure its continuation and growth. The facility was

renamed Burrus Memorial Hospital (in memory of the doctor's parents). A Board of Trustees was appointed. The Nursing School gained state approval, and the growth that had been interrupted by the Depression began again. By the mid-1930s, the hospital had a physician in charge of radiation, a registered nurse in the emergency room, two lab technicians, a dietitian, and a secretary.

In the early 1940s, the Board of Trustees appealed to the federal government to build a new facility, but was unsuccessful due to the needs of other hospitals providing services related to World War II. In 1944 Burrus Memorial merged with Guilford General Hospital, another High Point hospital in a large frame house. The combined hospital was called High Point Memorial Hospital, and patients could choose either site. The Women's Hospital Guild formed the following year.

After a successful building campaign in the late 1940s, High Point Memorial opened a new 100-bed facility in 1950. A concrete walkway connected it to the old Burrus Memorial, which by then had 80 beds in use.

The 1950s proved expansive—a modern nurses dormitory and classroom opened in 1954, and a $1.3 million expansion was begun in 1958. High Point Memorial grew along with High Point. The town of 6,500 people, which had 12 hospital beds in 1904,

High Point Memorial Hospital, 1950

High Point Regional Hospital, 1996

up with community leaders in 1993 to open the Community Clinic of High Point for the region's medically indigent. In 1995 the hospital developed a new department—the Community Health Institute—expressly dedicated to improving the health of the entire service area.

In 1904 High Point's hospital did not have the "tools" to help area residents live a healthier life. Today it has vaccinations, risk assessments, preventive diet and exercise plans, and highly sophisticated early detection and intervention techniques—all designed to help residents of High Point and its surrounding communities avoid the catastrophic illnesses and injuries that plagued previous generations. Together, High Point Regional Hospital, and everyone in its service area, can embark on a journey of improving the quality of health and life. ∞

had grown to a city of nearly 40,000 with 243 hospital beds.

In every decade, the Hospital Guild's generous donations have increased the availability of both technologically advanced care and comfort for patients. A Guild donation provided a mobile X-ray unit for the operating room, the first in North Carolina. In 1966 Guild funding purchased three neurosurgery air drills, another "first" in the state. Guild donations furnished air-conditioning for the hospital and the nursing school, and paid for the first full-time chaplain and first social worker. The Hospital Guild's pledge of $75,000 for a 1967 expansion was the first and largest donation to that building campaign.

A final expansion in 1971 shifted the focus not only of the entrance (from 1950s art deco to modern) but also gave the hospital improved diagnostic capabilities—a new clinical laboratory, an enlarged X-ray department, and a specialized coronary care unit. But before the decade was out, the Board of Trustees was looking for more space, and considering building a replacement for the hospital that had been added on to decade after decade.

The site for the new facility created a citywide controversy, but in 1982 the trustees decided to stay at the original Boulevard location. Ground was broken in June of that year, and with the support of the Duke

Endowment, a $500,000 gift from the Hospital Guild, and over $10 million from local contributions, the new High Point Regional Hospital came into being. George Bush, then vice president of the United States, presided at the ribbon cutting on November 8, 1985, when construction was almost complete.

On moving day, January 8, 1986, patients were brought to the new building through an underground tunnel connecting it to the old hospital. The tunnel proved so convenient that it is still used to transport patients to and from The Phillips Cancer Pavilion to receive radiation therapy.

As the twentieth century draws to a close, High Point Regional's full-service hospital treats over 90,000 patients each year from the city and surrounding counties. What started as a small community hospital has emerged as a health care leader for the region. High Point Regional continues to grow in response to the needs of the region, while forming collaborative partnerships that enhance the health and well-being of the people of High Point. The hospital and the Urban Ministry teamed

Mr. Andrew Corbett began working at the hospital in 1910 and remained for 73 years.

One of the first things most people do in the morning is to put on a pair of socks. Twenty million dozen pairs of socks a year are made in America by Adams-Millis, the largest producer of socks in the world.

Now a division of Sara Lee Corporation, Adams-Millis is headquartered in High Point, where the company began almost a century ago.

James Henry Millis was a successful businessman when he went into partnership with John Hampton Adams to start High Point Hosiery Mills in 1904. Producing only 200 dozen pairs of socks a day initially, the company grew quickly, so that by the time of Millis's death in 1913, it was believed to have the largest payroll of any company in High Point.

Millis was a stockholder and director of other companies, including banks, a wholesale food company, a savings and loan, and several furniture companies. Instrumental in High Point's emergence as a furniture center, he was also chairman of the Guilford County board of commissioners for 10 years. After his death, it was written that "he was big-hearted and sympathetic and very helpful to the entire citizenship of his community" and that his children inherited their father's business sagacity "as well as his other splendid qualities."

Under his sons, Henry Albion Millis and James Edward Millis, the tradition of community leadership continued, as did the growth of the hosiery company. More plants were built and acquired, and Adams-Millis Corporation was listed on the New York Stock Exchange in 1928.

In the late 1920s, the company was pioneering the use of rayon for ladies' hosiery at a new plant in High Point. The business was so profitable that the company came through the stock market crash of 1929 and the Depression unharmed. With the invention of nylon in 1938, the company immediately switched to making nylon stockings. But the United States' entry into World War II soon deprived women of their nylons. The fabric

was needed for military parachutes, and ladies' hosiery was once again made of rayon.

War created a military demand for men's socks. Adams-Millis sold 37 million pairs to the armed forces, more than any other company in the United States.

The third generation of the Millis family, named for his grandfather James Henry Millis, took over after the war. Jim Millis, who was a fighter pilot in the war, had worked in the plants during the summers of his high school and college years. Hot steam was used to shape socks, and he vividly recalls performing that job in the years before the mills were air-conditioned and before the steam was contained in the shaping machines.

In his 42 years at the helm, Jim Millis grew the company to an employer of 3,600 people. Eight more hosiery plants were acquired, and in the 1960s and 1970s, the company diversified into computer products, aluminum die casting, and covered and textured yarn manufacturing. Like many large corporations, it moved in and out of the diversification phase fairly quickly before deciding to "stick to its knitting." The company then acquired two hosiery companies, Silverknit and Maro.

Since 1960, Adams-Millis had been producing socks for Hanes,

an operation which grew so large that in 1988, the board of directors decided it would be in the best long-term interests of stockholders to sell the company to Sara Lee Corporation, which had acquired the Hanes companies several years before. At this major turning point in Adams-Millis's history, annual sales had exceeded $200 million.

"It was a very emotional decision," Jim Millis said. "We produced and marketed hosiery for the whole family, and we were a family—management and employees." Like the Millis family, several generations of hundreds of families had spent their lives working for the company.

The fortune that the Millis family made continues to benefit the High Point community, through the James H. and Jesse E. Millis Foundation, which was created shortly after the sale.

James Henry Millis

After Adams-Millis was acquired by Sara Lee Corporation, the company began the process of consolidating its manufacturing operations in Mt. Airy, High Point, and Kernersville, North Carolina, and Barnwell, South Carolina. Now, a distribution center in Kernersville serves all the plants, and the company's corporate offices are located in a new building on Eastchester Drive.

Some 2,300 people are employed in making socks that are sold under many brand names, including Hanes, Hanes Her Way, Champion, Just My Size, and Spalding. Private label socks sold by Polo, The Gap, Bass, Hot Socks, and other specialty retailers are also Adams-Millis products.

In fact, a major trend in the industry in recent years is an emphasis on brand names. Through most of their history, socks were just socks. Hanes was a leader in getting consumers to ask for socks by name. As new brands of sportswear, underwear, and women's sheer hosiery were added by the Sara Lee Hanes divisions, socks were added to the lines that consumers knew and trusted. Whatever brand name they carry, and

whether they are sold in discount stores, department stores, outlet stores, or through direct mail catalogs, all of Sara Lee's socks are made by Adams-Millis.

In becoming part of the Hanes tradition at Sara Lee, Adams-Millis joined a company that was early to recognize that, by and large, women buy the socks for the whole family. In the 1960s, Hanes changed the way women bought pantyhose, by packaging them in plastic eggs and conveniently placing them in grocery stores and drugstores. Ever since, the company's marketing strategies have been geared to the preferences of women, no matter who will wear the socks.

In the 1990s, Adams-Millis is riding the tide of America's increasingly casual lifestyle. The socks that the man of 1904 put on each morning were black—and black was the only color that the old High Point Hosiery Mills turned out.

John Hampton Adams

The man of today has business socks in several shades, patterned or colorful socks for casual wear, athletic socks of various lengths and weights for a variety of sports and exercise activities, and perhaps some Christmas or other themed socks, just for fun. And socks are a growing aspect of women's liberation, increasingly turning up at social events and in the office. Not surprisingly, Adams-Millis was the first Sara Lee division to institute casual Fridays. Everybody wears socks! ∞

James Edward Millis

Shown in this artist's rendering, High Point Bank and Trust Company relocated its headquarters to a new building on North Main Street in 1963, and held a grand opening remembered by many as the social event of the year.

Hervie N. Williard, president of High Point Savings and Trust from 1937 until 1959, was widely admired as a man of vision, tolerance, and understanding.

The bank opened as High Point Savings and Trust Company in September, 1905, in a small office in the old Elwood Hotel building on South Main Street. These rented accommodations served until 1929, when the bank moved to 111 North Main Street. The original vault, decorated and gilded in the style of the early part of the century, was used at both locations, then stored until the bank's 90th anniversary, when it was painstakingly restored and displayed.

The Rev. Hilliard moved to Asheville in 1913, leaving the presidency to J. Elwood Cox, who served in that capacity until 1933. Between the bank's founding and the Depression years, its assets had grown from $137,000 to $703,800. Ed L. Ragan led the bank in the four-year transition from post-Depression slump to pre-World War II prosperity.

In 1937 Hervie N. Williard, who had 18 years of service with the bank by then, was elected president. He spearheaded growth that increased the size of the bank almost fifteenfold in his 18 years at the helm. By 1945 the bank had total resources of more than $8 million. During his tenure, the bank opened its first branch in 1956, at 441 South Main Street. Hervie Williard was widely admired as a man of vision, tolerance, and understanding, and when he died suddenly of a heart attack in 1959, the entire community mourned. Along with the phenomenal growth over which he presided, he gave the bank a living legacy. His daughter, Lynn Williard McInnis, served the bank in executive capacities for 40 years, rising to become chairman of the board. His grandson, Robert H. McInnis, joined the bank in 1974, became president in 1986, and has been chairman of the board since his mother's death in 1989. Also, his granddaughter, Elizabeth M. Nooe, was elected to the board in 1990.

Fred W. Alexander became president after Hervie Williard's death and made the bank North Carolina's 11th largest in his 27 years of leadership. The hometown bank was still

In 1905 a group of civic leaders, envisioning a bright future for their entrepreneurial and industrious city, met to organize a locally owned and controlled bank. More than 90 years later, High Point Bank and Trust Company is still the hometown bank—the largest single city bank in North Carolina and one of the largest local banks in the state.

The seven original stockholders were the Rev. S. H. Hilliard Jr., J. W. Harris, Fred N. Tate, Dred Peacock, H. W. Frazier, D. N. Welborn, and A. J. Rickle. They and the other members of the first board of directors made up a veritable "Who's Who" of prominent High Point families—J. E. Kirkman, W. G. Bradshaw, F. M. Pickett, D. A. Stanton, J. Elwood Cox, W. J. McAnally, R. Ragan, M. B. Smith, J. J. Welch, A. J. Dodamead, G. H. Kearns, J. P. Redding, C. M. Hauser, J. W. Sechrest, H. A. White, and A. Sherrod. Hilliard, a former pastor of Washington Street Methodist Church (later Wesley Memorial Methodist Church), was elected first president.

Under Fred W. Alexander's leadership, the bank grew to be the 11th largest in North Carolina.

High Point Savings and Trust when Alexander assumed the presidency. The board of directors received permission from the North Carolina State Banking Commission to change the name to High Point Bank and Trust Company in 1962.

The following year the headquarters office moved to its new building at 312 North Main Street, a 21,000-square-foot facility that has since been expanded. The grand opening in May, 1963, is remembered by many as the social event of the year. The bank's loyal customers turned out en masse, lining up on the sidewalks, eager for a look at the new banking office. Every member of the staff was on hand to greet them.

The Fairfield and Westchester branch offices were opened during Alexander's presidency, and by the time of his retirement in 1986, the bank's resources were listed at more than $325 million.

In the late 1980s, Robert H. McInnis initiated a $3 million expansion to the main office. The 41,000-square-foot addition includes a handsome tri-level lobby for the commercial department, and three floors of offices for loan and trust operations and other tenants.

Since 1989 F. David Hall has been president of the bank, and since 1990 the bank has been structured as a wholly owned subsidiary of the High Point Bank Corporation. In 1995 the Jamestown branch of the bank moved to a new building on Guilford College Road—on the exact spot where Hervie N. Williard and his wife had made their home.

Through its entire history, High Point Bank has been intimately linked with High Point's homegrown businesses. It is known for having helped many get started and for helping them survive through hard times. Its presidents have been bankers who would extend credit on a handshake, so well do they know their customers. It's a bank that almost never advertises, because its hometown atmosphere sells its services. The High Point community repays its hometown bank with intense loyalty.

In today's environment of interstate banking and mergers, High Point Bank and Trust is a rarity—thriving and profitable—a local bank with local management and local customers. ∞

In the late 1980s the bank underwent a significant expansion under the direction of Robert H. McInnis.

"Sunday Afternoon, 1912, High Point, North Carolina" by M. Motley Godwin. *Courtesy The High Point Museum Archives.*

High Point residents have been talking on the phone since 1895, when the High Point Telephone Exchange was established. In 1899, when Jesse F. Hayden and T. J. Finch bought the exchange, it had only 60 customers.

A native of Davidson County and a graduate of Trinity College (now Duke University), Hayden was a gifted inventor and entrepreneur who looked ahead to the new technologies at the turn of the century.

Hayden was early to see the potential of long-distance service. After building the Thomasville Exchange in 1898, and buying the High Point Exchange, he built his first toll line, connecting the two towns. Toll lines to Greensboro and Winston-Salem followed.

In 1905 Hayden incorporated North State Telephone Company. In 1909 the company purchased a building on West Washington Street in High Point and equipped it with a Stromberg-Carlson manual switchboard, to which Hayden added his own patented improvements. North State was the first telephone company in North Carolina to use harmonic, party-line ringing.

During those early years, North State competed with Southern Bell. Bell tried to

The "Hello Girls" at this manually operated switchboard connected callers in the High Point Exchange in the early 1900s.

Through the years, North State has kept abreast of the many advancements in communications technology in providing modern, useful services to the public.

attract customers with free trial service, but in six years it had signed up less than 300 subscribers. When the United States became involved in World War I, the federal government ordered all competing phone companies to connect their toll lines, and Bell was forced to link North State's lines to its own switchboards in surrounding cities. Without exclusive use of its own lines, Bell decided to relinquish High Point's business. In 1919 Bell sold its telephone system to North State, bringing a 20-year rivalry to an end.

Hayden then turned his attention to setting up an automatic telephone exchange, which would eliminate the need for the operators, or "Hello Girls," who manually connected callers to the numbers they were calling. He contracted with two brothers, Robbins and Tom A. Tilden, who had installed an automatic exchange at a Naval base. The new equipment was installed in the building North State had bought from Southern Bell on College Street. On July 10, 1920, High Point became the first city in the state (and one of the first in the country) to have automatic dialing.

Jesse Hayden was elected president of the company in 1934, a position he held until

his death, in 1952. By its 50th anniversary year, 1955, North State could claim over 25,000 telephones, handling 180,500 local calls and 38,000 toll calls a day. Hayden's widow, Velva Green Hayden, who had been active in the company since their marriage in 1902, succeeded him as president and chairman of the board. She served until 1973, when Robbins Tilden was elected. North State is now headed by the Haydens' grandson, Royster M. Tucker Jr.

From Touch-Tone™ phones to cellular service, fax, voice mail, pagers, Internet services, modems, and fiber optics, North State customers have access to all the benefits of modern telecommunications technology. In the 1990s subscribers were surfing the Internet and driving down the North Carolina Information Highway, the network of high-speed voice, video, and data transmission that North State has helped build. In 1995, its 100th year, North State ranked among the 25 largest telephone companies in the United States, yet its rates for local service are the lowest in North Carolina. ⌒

Wachovia Bank of North Carolina

During the century in which High Point grew to become the furniture manufacturing and marketing capital of the world, Wachovia has been a strong partner in the start-up and growth of many of its businesses. The Winston-Salem-based bank, in the early stages of its own steady growth, opened one of its first branches in High Point, then a town of 9,000 with a strong concentration of textile and furniture entrepreneurs.

Wachovia gets its unusual name from the Moravian settlers of the nearby town of Salem. It is the Latin form of "Wachau," which is what the settlers called their tract of land in Piedmont North Carolina. The bank began in Salem in 1866, moved to the neighboring town of Winston in 1879, and merged with the young Wachovia Loan and Trust Company in 1911, two years before Winston and Salem were formally joined.

Wachovia established a High Point branch in 1906, and in 1996 has five branches in the High Point-Archdale-Jamestown area, with a local governing board headed by George

Erath. The main office at the corner of Main and Kivett was opened in 1964 and underwent an unexpected renovation 20 years later. On Valentine's Day, 1984, a fire started in a wastebasket in one of the offices on the banking floor. The old Biltmore Hotel was burning at the same time, and when the Wachovia alarm sounded, firefighters assumed it was the hotel fire. The fire closed the bank for only one day. With a trailer in the parking lot and some operations moved upstairs, business continued while the lobby was rebuilt.

Wachovia offers a full line of banking services and products to businesses and individuals. A $45-billion bank in 1996, it has been aggressive in investing in the technologies of the Information Age, such as image technology that enables commercial customers to receive their cancelled checks on easily stored compact discs, Electronic Data Interchange services for precisely timed payments and fund transfers, on-line information services, and a variety of PC products.

The bank has been a leader in responding to consumer preferences. Customers have the choice of going into the bank, using a branch or stand-alone Automated Teller Machine, calling 1-800-WACHOVIA to speak with a telephone banker, 24 hours a day, seven days a week, or dialing another toll-free number for recorded information.

"We recognize that people want banking services in different ways," said Pete Callahan, who became Wachovia's city executive for High Point in 1995. "We can interact with customers in any way they want."

The High Point operation has made more loans under the Neighborhood Revitalization Program than any Wachovia office in the state. This program, introduced in 1989, relaxes traditional underwriting requirements to enable lower-income families to obtain mortgages. "Getting people to own homes enhances the whole community," Callahan said.

Similarly, the High Point office has been aggressive in making loans to women, minorities, and small business owners. Through the Small Business Loan Program, credit is extended to businesses which do not meet traditional criteria, but do have viable business plans and a commitment to financial planning.

Beyond banking services, Wachovia is a generous contributor to the development of High Point's quality of life. ∞

When Larry and Ann Miller first entered the old Bouldin family homestead on Archdale Road, they were taken by surprise. The young couple had spent months searching for a property suitable for a bed and breakfast inn. They'd searched from Maine to Maryland without success, and in late 1992 they stopped in the High Point area. What the Millers found was a finely crafted, commodious house, looking not much different from when it was built, circa 1915.

The Millers bought the house from Ollie Bouldin, the wife of one of the seven children raised there. Bouldins had owned hundreds of acres in the area since the 1880s. According to family lore, two brothers, David and Myron Bouldin, built identical houses a mile apart. When David married, his wife didn't want to live in the country, so he sold his house—the current Bouldin House—to his brother. Myron lived in the house, and passed it down to his son, Joseph, a tobacco farmer, past Randolph County Sheriff, and used car dealer.

Joseph's sister Irene, born in 1919, lives several houses down from the Bouldin House. She remembers when the house was part of a thriving farm, with orchards, gardens, and livestock, as well as tobacco fields. The women of the household prepared three meals a day for up to 20 people who worked on the farm. In bed at night, in what is now called the Warm Morning Room, the last thing Irene would see before dropping off to sleep was the flickering light of the fires burning in the tobacco drying barns.

The last tobacco crops were pulled in about 1970, and eventually most of the acreage was sold. Widowed in the 1970s, Ollie Bouldin lived in the big house alone, until she decided to sell in 1992. She and many other Bouldin family members live nearby and have watched the Millers lovingly restore the homestead, giving it a bold new exterior color scheme—yellow wood siding and a red roof.

Larry Miller did much of the interior renovation himself, stripping and refinishing the paneling, wainscoting, fireplaces, mouldings, and banisters. Much of the wood in the house was cut from the property, and milled locally by the English family.

The Millers had been buying their personal furniture in Thomasville for several years before moving to North Carolina, and when it came time to furnish the bedrooms, dining room, and sitting rooms, they bought everything locally. The spacious rooms in the house accommodate large-scale furniture and dramatic colors. The new look of the Bouldin House, which opened as a bed and breakfast in July, 1994, is what the Millers call "sophisticated country; casual and relaxed, yet elegant."

Most of the guests, who come from all over the country, are people shopping for furniture. After long days trekking through showrooms, they relax on the big front porch, or warm themselves by the fireplace in every room, or join other guests for a game of Pictionary in the sitting room. Breakfasts are sumptuous and not at all countrified. Puffed pastry filled with tarragon-seasoned eggs, omelettes filled with Boursin and pesto, toasted pecan buttermilk pancakes, and oatmeal current scones are some of the Millers' specialties.

The guest book indicates how visitors feel about the Bouldin House. "Excellent," "lovely," and "wonderful" are the usual comments. When a more restrained guest wrote "very pleasant," Larry Miller was crushed.

While becoming an innkeeper, Miller discovered a genuine interest in historic preservation. "I think the house has been given another 100 years of life, without a doubt," he said proudly. ☙

This early photograph, circa 1920, shows how very little the old Bouldin homeplace has changed from the time it was a working tobacco farm.

Today, after two years of sensitive renovation aimed at preserving the integrity of its foursquare heritage, the Bouldin House Bed & Breakfast offers travelers a warm and wonderful respite.

Thomas Built Buses

Before there were buses, there were streetcars; and before there was Thomas Built Buses, there was Perley A. Thomas Car Works.

Perley A. Thomas, born in Canada in 1874, got his early experience in building streetcars in Detroit. He came to High Point in 1910 to be chief engineer of Southern Car Company. When that company ceased operations in 1916, Thomas started his own car works.

The first wood-and-steel streetcars carrying the Thomas name were transported on railroad flatcars to nearby Durham and faraway Detroit, Miami Beach, and New Orleans. The famous "Streetcar Named Desire" in New Orleans, immortalized in Tennessee Williams' drama of the same name, was a Thomas Built car.

Perley Thomas's four children—Willard, Norman, Melva, and Mary—all entered the business. A family story is illustrative of Perley Thomas's legendary insistence on quality and service: It came to "Mr. P.A.'s" attention that one of 10 streetcars shipped to Miami was missing a door-opening device. He immediately dispatched his son Norman

to Florida, with orders to catch the next train back. Any ideas Norman may have had about a tropical vacation were squelched. He delivered the missing part and headed home to High Point without ever seeing a beach.

By the late 1920s, it was obvious that streetcars were a dying industry. As cars, buses, and trolley coaches began to replace the old streetcars, P. A. Thomas turned to manufacturing trolley coaches. The times did not favor him; competition was stiff, and the sluggish Depression economy reduced the demand for coaches.

During the Depression, Mr. P.A. used his well-honed woodworking skills to make ends meet. The beautifully carved mantelpieces and paneling in some of High Point's fine old homes are his handiwork.

In 1934 Thomas learned that the state of North Carolina was soliciting bids for school bus bodies. His low bid to build several hundred of the new style, canvas-roofed buses was accepted. This order put the company into full production, enabled Mr. P.A. to turn a $10,000 profit, and set the future direction of the business.

Thomas turned out school buses for

North Carolina, and for the other southeastern states over the next decade, until bus production was suspended during the Second World War. During the war years Thomas produced mobile arms shops for the military. These units were mounted on the back of Army trucks and were used for supplying and repairing rifles and other small combat weapons.

When bus production resumed after the war, Thomas launched a nationwide expansion program, with distributors throughout the United States. The line of 30, 36, and 48-passenger buses was expanded to include larger buses and custom-built models for prison buses, church and activity buses, chick delivery buses, and transit buses. Thomas went international during the 1960s, setting up subsidiaries in Canada, Peru, and Ecuador.

In the 1990s Thomas Built Buses is one of North Carolina's largest exporters, and one of the world's largest producers of buses. While its main product continues to be school buses, Thomas also makes transit and commercial buses, and has built prototype electric buses. With manufacturing facilities in three locations, Thomas turns out 36 buses a day in High Point, 18 a day in Woodstock, Ontario, and 3 each day in Monterey, Mexico. Some 1,600 people work for the company.

Since more stringent federal safety regulations were established in 1977, Thomas has been at the forefront of meeting and exceeding safety standards for school buses. Some of the newer models have a "flat-nose" front which provides much improved visibility for the driver, and engines in the rear to reduce noise in the driver area.

The company has also worked to produce sturdy, reliable products at competitive prices. A school bus that will stand up to 15,000 miles per year of stop-and-go use for 15 years costs less than a luxury automobile. The top-of-the-line streetcars Thomas manufactured in its early years were priced at $7,000. The price of a Thomas Built school

The Thomas Saf-T-Liner-ER is the finest rear-engine school coach on the road today. Its outstanding visibility and safety features have made this model popular with school districts across the U.S. and Canada. The unit pictured below is first of 2,002 delivered to the state of South Carolina in 1995. This was the largest single school bus order in history.

One of 100 streetcars delivered to the city of New Orleans in October of 1924.
The famous "Streetcar Named Desire" was one of these P. A. Thomas Cars.

bus in the 1990s starts at $45,000. One thing that hasn't changed over the years, according to John W. Thomas III, president and CEO, is the time it takes to manufacture a vehicle for mass transportation. It took five months to build a streetcar. It takes five months to schedule and build a bus.

In 1994 Thomas Built Buses got its largest order, the largest single order in the history of the school bus industry. The state of South Carolina ordered 2,002 buses, a $103,312,000 contract.

Under the fourth generation of Thomas family management, the company looks to a bright future for school buses and opportunities for diversification. Trends that spell a growing market for school buses include the "baby boomlet" that began in the late 1970s, the millions of mothers of school-age children in the workforce, the increasing consolidation of city and suburban school districts, and a continuing concern for replacing older equipment with newer and safer buses.

In April 1996, members of the Thomas family and senior management, with the assistance of Berkshire Partners, a Boston-based investment group, acquired ownership of the company. As part of the buyout, John W. Thomas III was named chief executive officer in addition to his duties as president. His father, John W. Thomas Jr., continues as chairman of the board of directors. ∞

This restored 1940 Thomas School Bus was owned by Iredell County Schools in North Carolina. In July of 1996, Thomas offered to trade the school system a brand new Activity Bus for the antique. The county accepted the offer and the company is now the proud owner of a piece of its history.

Harriss & Covington Hosiery Mills, Inc.

Julius Ward Harriss and his son-in-law, W. Comer Covington, founded Harriss and Covington Hosiery Mills in 1920. While their plant at 300 Oak Street was under construction, the company operated from the second floor of the old Henley Paper Company building on South Hamilton Street. Ladies' mercerized cotton stockings were the first products, but after a few years the company began to manufacture men's hosiery exclusively. Sales topped $1 million for the first time in 1928.

Wartime changed the workforce. While most young men were serving their country, women and older men did the knitting, dyeing, boarding, pairing, and packaging. The socks they produced then were for servicemen, and the predominant colors were Army green and black.

Nylon and Orlon began to replace silk, rayon, and acetate after the war, and Harriss and Covington was one of the first hosiery mills to make use of the new synthetic fibers. The socks were sold through agents in New York to national chain stores, under the stores' own labels. In 1966 J. Welch Harriss and Harriss Covington, the sons of the founders of the company, decided on a different marketing strategy. They set up their own sales office in New York. In one day the company lost 40 percent of the sales that had been handled by independent agents, but over the long run, dealing directly with customers proved to be a wise and winning move.

The company's philosophy of extraordinary customer service, achieved through centralized operations, carefully managed growth, and investment in state-of-the-art technology, blossomed under the leadership of Harriss Covington. The Oak Street facility was expanded several times, until there was no more room to expand. In the late 1960s, Harriss and Covington bought 19 acres on the outskirts of High Point and began construction of a modern, air-conditioned, one-level plant. The facility on East Green Street Extension opened in 1970, and now houses knitting, seaming, dyeing, boarding, pairing and packaging operations, as well as corporate offices and sales functions, which were moved here from New York.

Today Harriss and Covington produces a full line of men's dress, casual, and athletic hosiery as well as women's casual and athletic socks. The socks are sold under a variety of branded names, including Foot-Joy, Fila, and FootLocker. Woolworth's has been a customer for over 60 years, and socks made by Harriss and Covington are also sold by J.C. Penney, Melville, and other national chains.

Exceptional customer service, a strong commitment to its 320 employees, and a reputation for ethical business practice and civic philanthropy continue to characterize Harriss and Covington Hosiery Mills under the fourth generation of family ownership and leadership.

"We continue to pour capital into modern equipment. We pride ourselves on what we happily do for our customers and employees. We give away five percent of our profits every year to community causes. We're committed to the hosiery business and to controlled growth. We'd rather be good than big," said Edward H. "Ned" Covington, who has been the company president since 1985. ❧

President Ned Covington, stands in front of a portrait of his father, J. Harriss Covington, who, along with J. Welch Harriss, led Harriss and Covington Hosiery Mills in the 1960s and 1970s.

Harriss and Covington Hosiery Mills Vice President Darrell Frye inspects operations in the company's knitting room.

On a mild October evening in 1924, High Point's leading merchants met for a banquet at the Sheraton Hotel to form a new association. Their discussion resulted in the 1925 establishment of the High Point Merchants Association. Its goals included fostering a friendly feeling among commercial interests, abating trade abuses and injurious practices, and protecting the public against such ills as "impure foods, mis-branded articles, short weights and measures, and false and fraudulent advertising."

For most of its history, however, the Association's main purpose has been to provide credit reports. The organization, which began with fewer than a dozen members, has grown to include more than 530 members. That growth is very closely tied to the growth of personal credit.

"It's the most important thing we could do; it's valuable to both grantors and consumers," says Danny M. Courtney, who has been president of the Association since 1976.

As an example, he cites the August, 1995, opening of the Oak Hollow Mall. All the anchor stores at the mall offered credit card promotions, and in that month alone the Merchants Association processed 42,186 credit reports.

Sharon Smith, vice president of the Association, has worked for the organization since 1968, and remembers when credit reporting was a manual operation. "We used to be in an old, dilapidated building over the Princess Cafe, next to a pool hall," she recalls. "We'd go and get the reports from the filing cabinet and read them over the phone."

As many as 20 employees were needed to handle the 200 or so credit reports a day. Now, when reporting is done via computer terminals linked to databases, two people can handle the usual load of about 1,500 reports

The Hamilton-Wrenn entrance to the High Point Merchants Association building

a day. And in the computer age, credit reporting goes on, automatically, virtually every hour of the day and night, in contrast to the time when a credit bureau employee had to work on Saturdays to accommodate requests from automobile dealers. Still another change is the Equifax service. A credit report on a shopper, visiting High Point from anywhere in the United States, can be accessed in seconds, through the credit bureau's link to a nationwide database.

Another part of the Association's work is interviewing people who have been refused credit, showing them their credit files, and correcting any erroneous information.

Since 1978, the Association has provided a collection service for members. Over the years, it has collected more than $11 million in outstanding debts. A residential mortgage service is also offered.

Christmas is the season when the Merchants Association makes a gift to High Point of two of the community s favorite traditions—the decorations on Main Street and the Christmas parade. The 18-foot-long "teardrop" decorations that hang on poles

were designed especially for High Point, and always evoke favorable reactions. The parade, held on the Tuesday night before Thanksgiving, has grown to be one of the largest in the state.

In 1995 the Merchants Association responded to requests for a clock on Main Street by installing a chiming street clock in front of its building. The distinctive time-piece was custom-made in Cincinnati. It is "two-faced," as is the Merchants Association building, a former dry cleaning establishment, now remodeled and expanded with distinctly different front and rear facades. ∞

In 1951 High Point's Centennial Parade passed by Rose Furniture Company's store on South Main Street.

Rose Furniture Company was founded in 1925 by O. V. Kester, who decided to go into business for himself, having worked previously in furniture manufacturing. The store's first location was next to a rose garden on English Street in the West End—and Kester named his business for those neighboring flowers.

The store moved downtown in 1933, next to the old High Point Hardware store on South Main Street. It was managed there for several years by O.V.'s sons, Vance and Gene. In 1958 the brothers built a new facility on South Elm Street, which was used for 28 years. In 1986 Rose Furniture moved to its present location at 916 Finch Avenue. With its 1994 addition, the building has 166,000 square feet of space. The company also maintains five warehouses and a clearance center on South Main Street.

W. V. "Bill" Kester Jr. has been president since he was 27 years old. He and his brothers worked in the business from an early age—first dusting furniture and sweeping floors, and then working in the warehouses and on the delivery trucks when they reached college age. Besides Bill, six Kester family members now are involved in the business—Bill's brothers Buck and Tom, Bill's sons Tripp and Todd, his cousin David, and his nephew Tommy.

Furniture retailing is closely tied to the economy as a whole, but Rose survived the Depression, when most people couldn't afford to buy new furniture, and World War II, when most raw materials were going to the war effort. It grew to be one of the largest retail furniture

O. V. Kester founded Rose Furniture Company in 1925.

For 28 years Rose Furniture satisfied its many customers from this location on South Elm Street.

operations, 55th in the country by volume of business. In 1995 Rose employed 65 salespeople and carried stock from some 500 furniture manufacturers.

Some 3,000 people visit the store every week, from all over the country and from many foreign countries. Rose has done business with presidents and kings. Rose operates a catalog business, too.

Bill Kester attributes the company's success to offering a wide variety of furniture and accessories, by top quality manufacturers, with good pricing and good service. ∞

In 1994 Rose Furniture Company added 166,000 square feet of space to its Finch Avenue location.

Reflections of the Past

Ilderton
Dodge-Chrysler-Plymouth

In the mid-1920s, Horace G. Ilderton was the top Dodge salesman in the Southeast. He worked for a dealership in Charleston, South Carolina, and he was invited to the Dodge headquarters in Greensboro to receive an award. While he was in North Carolina, he was offered a management position, at either the Greensboro or the High Point Dodge dealership. He chose High Point.

Ilderton bought the High Point dealership from its owner, a Major Faison, and established it as Horace G. Ilderton, Inc. on October 26, 1926. At first only Dodge cars and trucks were sold, but shortly thereafter Chrysler bought the Dodge Brothers' business, and introduced the Plymouth. Ilderton was a Dodge-Plymouth dealer until 1981, when it became Dodge-Chrysler-Plymouth.

In 1933 Ilderton acquired the Sinclair Oil Co. distributorship, which sold kerosene fuel oil and industrial oils and gas. This put him in a position to take part in the lowering of High Point's railroad tracks. In 1935 Eddie Knox, mayor of the City of High Point, set about remedying the great divide caused by the tracks. Blythe Brothers of Charlotte dug the huge ditch through the city to lower the

Ilderton's as it looked in 1932, with Dodge "Straight Eights" and "Senior Sixes"

tracks, and Ilderton got the contract for all the oil, gas, and grease used on the project. This big contract enabled him to buy two new trucks to service the job, and to establish Ilderton Oil Company. The railroad job was completed in 1940, and the bridge over the railroad tracks was named for the mayor, Knox Bridge. Ilderton Oil later became an Amoco distributorship, and is now operated by Clarence Ilderton.

During World War II, the federal government took control of automobile manufacturing, and sales of new cars were frozen. Many franchise dealers closed, but those like Ilderton that stayed in business were ordered to put their new automobiles into storage. Ilderton had 50 new vehicles in stock when the edict was issued in 1942, and

from then until 1946, only people with special permits could buy a new car. They included doctors, mail carriers, and certain workers in industries essential to the war effort. The government paid automobile dealers one percent per month of the value of their new car stock to enable them to weather the restrictions.

After the war, the demand for new cars was enormous. Getting enough stock to meet the demand was the problem then.

Carey Ilderton Sr. joined his father in the business in January, 1946, after military service in the war. He felt that it was time to expand. The dealership was still in its original location, at the corner of Commerce and Willowbrook (now Elm). In 1950 they constructed the building on South Main Street in which the dealership is still located. Adjoining properties were purchased over the years, and Ilderton's now covers about 10 acres fronting on South Main.

After Horace Ilderton's death in 1971, Carey Ilderton Sr. became the dealer and co-owner with his sister, Gloria Ilderton

For over 30 years, the Ilderton dealership has been the recipient of many national awards for both sales volume and customer service and satisfaction.

Ilderton Conversion Company specializes in building and selling vehicles adapted for the physically handicapped and converting vans for mass transit.

Rochelle, and brother, Clarence Ilderton, Sr. Carey Ilderton eventually purchased their shares and today owns the business with three of his sons, Carey Jr., Tim, and Steve. All are active in the business.

In 1972, before almost anybody had heard of van conversions, Ilderton got into the business of building and selling vehicles adapted for the physically handicapped. Now Ilderton Conversion Co. has its own building with six full-time associates. It is one of the few businesses of its kind in North Carolina, and draws customers from Pennsylvania to Florida.

In about 1980, Ilderton became the first dealer to provide vans for the twice-yearly furniture market. By then the market had grown to a size at which the city of High Point and the Southern Furniture Manufacturers Association were working out ways of transporting buyers from outlying parking lots to the downtown showrooms. Ilderton's now furnishes up to 50 vehicles during each market.

For over 30 years, Ilderton's has been the recipient of many national awards for both sales volume and customer service and satisfaction. The principals in the company have been active in the community and in their industry.

Horace Ilderton served as a member of the High Point City Council for 18 years and was active in state and local politics. Carey Ilderton Sr. has served on executive boards and is a past president of the North Carolina Automobile Dealers Association and has chaired the Dodge Dealer Council. He has been chairman of the Dodge Dealer Advertising Association for many years. In 1983 he was honored with the *Time* magazine's Quality Dealer Award. ✆

Ilderton's current location on South Main Street

"World's Largest Bureau" in Tate Park at Main and Church Streets, circa 1930. *Photo courtesy The High Point Museum Archives.*

Charles Lindbergh landed to a hero's welcome. Eleanor Roosevelt stopped for lunch. Will Rogers dropped in to raise money for drought-stricken farmers. Roy Acuff entertained at a rally for President Nixon. Elvis downed some doughnuts in his private plane after his last concert in Greensboro. Moshe Dayan flew in for a visit to the Top of the Mart in High Point.

Since May 28, 1927, when the largest crowd ever assembled in Guilford County witnessed its formal opening, the airport that serves central North Carolina, including High Point, Greensboro, Winston-Salem, and southern Virginia has been the region's transportation hub. By the mid-1990s, nearly four million people each year were taking off from or landing at Piedmont Triad International Airport. Another 4,000 people work at the airport, for more than 50 companies. The total annual impact of the airport on the local economy exceeds a billion dollars.

No city, county, state, or federal taxes are used to operate the airport. It is owned and managed by the Piedmont Triad Airport Authority, which was established by the North Carolina State Legislature in 1941. The Authority has a seven-member governing board, and a professional staff carries out the board's policies.

The airport is situated on 2,800 acres of green, gently rolling land near the center of the Triad. A 299-room Marriott Hotel is conveniently located on the property.

The two-level passenger terminal opened in 1982. Architects and Authority members studied modern European air terminals in preparation for designing the building, and its attractiveness and convenience are frequently noted by travelers. The terminal was built on acreage that had once been part of a dairy farm owned and operated by the University of North Carolina at Greensboro. The terminal is six times as large as the building it replaced, and includes 19 gates for aircraft departures.

Serving passengers on commercial flights is just one of the airport's important functions. Overnight air delivery services depend upon the airport. Federal Express, Airborne Express, and five other freight carriers operate from Piedmont Triad International Airport. Their planes fly overnight to cargo hubs in various part of the country for next-day delivery.

The airport is the home base to Trade Winds Airlines Incorporated which makes stops each day at the airport but doesn't carry a single passenger. Its L-1011 Tri-Star can carry up to 110,000 pounds of cargo, in 16,000 square feet of space. Textiles, footwear, pharmaceuticals, and electronics are the usual cargo, but Trade Winds has also transported heavy equipment and automobiles.

General aviation planes are very much part of the airport scene. Two full-service general aviation companies offer charter services, flying lessons, and sales and service of both used and new private airplanes. Piedmont Aviation specializes in Beechcraft airplanes; Atlantic Aero sells Cessna planes, and offers the largest jet charter operation in the Carolinas. Its flight school is one of the biggest in the state.

The airport is also known throughout the United States for a number of first-rate maintenance facilities. USAir, TIMCO (Triad International Maintenance Corporation), and Cessna Citation have maintenance hangars at the airport. Repair stations have become increasingly important in the airline industry, because of safety considerations, and because extending the life of their aircraft has become a pressing economic concern of airlines, freight services, and charter companies. TIMCO has the state-of-the-art equipment and technical capabilities to test and repair planes up to the size of DC-10s and 747s. ∞

Wyatt, Early, Harris & Wheeler

Wyatt Early Harris & Wheeler is High Point's largest and one of its oldest law firms. Located downtown in the historic Old Courthouse Building, the firm represents clients throughout the southeastern United States, including some of North Carolina's largest companies based in the Piedmont Triad.

To meet the challenges of the increasingly specialized legal profession, the attorneys and support staff are organized into broad practice areas which include business and corporate transactions, taxation, basic and complex litigation, bankruptcy, real estate, criminal law, estate planning and probate, family law, governmental, and environmental law.

Located in the heart of the "Furniture Capital of the World," Wyatt Early Harris & Wheeler made national headlines in 1992 when it established a new specialty department, the Furniture Practice Group, a first in the nation. Home furnishings manufacturers and suppliers have been clients since its beginning, and much of the firm's legal business comes from furniture, home furnishings, and related industries.

The firm, now consisting of 21 attorneys

Old Courthouse Building

and 25 support personnel, was founded in 1930 as the law office of Walter E. Crissman, Jr. He was joined in 1949 by Robert E. Bencini, Jr. Both later served with distinction as judges of the Superior Court and District Court of North Carolina. In 1959 the current executive partner, Frank Burkhead Wyatt, joined the firm, which now consists of Wyatt, William P. Harris, A. Doyle Early, Jr., William E. Wheeler, David B. Ashcraft, Kim W. Gallimore, Kim R. Bauman, Calvin B. Bryant, R. Bruce Laney, J. Brooks Reitzel, Jr.,

Charles A. Alt, Frederick G. Sawyer, James R. Hundley, Charles L. Cain, Thomas E. Terrell, Jr., Lee M. Cecil, Kevin L. Rochford, Ann E. Hanks, John D. Bryson, and Stanley F. Hammer.

In 1983 Wyatt Early Harris & Wheeler bought, renovated, and occupied the Old Guilford County Courthouse at 258 South Main Street, a building constructed in 1936 as North Carolina's 101st courthouse, which has been a most important part of High Point's governmental and political history. Designed by prominent local architects, Louis F. Voorhees and Eccles D. Everhart, it was the first county courthouse in the nation to be erected outside a county seat and is located on land formerly occupied by the home of Captain W. H. Snow, one of High Point's most prominent early settlers. The property, situated at the corner of Main and Green Streets, also faced directly onto the Fayetteville and Western Plank Road which extended from Fayetteville to Salem, and was the longest plank road, built in the United States during the mid 1800s.

Three floors of offices occupy the spaces which once were jail cells, courtrooms, judges' chambers, tax offices, sheriff's offices, and jury rooms.

Now listed on The National Register of Historic Places, the Old Courthouse Building retains its original Art Moderne exterior, notable for the three carved stone figures which represent what historically have been High Point's and Guilford County's major economic activities—furniture, textiles, and farming.

Although the law firm now operates with the latest in communication and computer technology, it remains comfortable in its historic setting, which underscores the high standards of quality for which Wyatt Early Harris & Wheeler is known. ∞

Seated, left to right: William E. Wheeler, Frank B. Wyatt, A. Doyle Early, Jr., William P. Harris
Standing, left to right: David B. Ashcraft, Thomas E. Terrell, J. Brooks Reitzel, Jr., Charles L. Cain, Stanley F. Hammer, Ann E. Hanks, R. Bruce Laney, Kim W. Gallimore, James R. Hundley, Kim R. Bauman
Not pictured: Calvin B. Bryant, Charles A. Alt, Kevin L. Rochford, John D. Bryson, Lee M. Cecil, Frederick G. Sawyer

Marlowe-Van Loan Corporation

Until the early 1930s the chemicals needed to process hosiery in High Point's mills came mainly from the Northeast. J. Wheeler Van Loan, the chief chemist for a New Jersey chemical company, and Thomas A. Marlowe, the company's southern region sales representative, saw an opportunity to serve the hosiery industry needs closer to home. In 1933 they formed their own specialty chemical business in High Point with a plant on South Hamilton Street.

The young company was aggressive in developing technologically advanced products and expanding its market base. Initially providing chemicals and dyestuffs for hosiery manufacturers in North and South Carolina, Marlowe-Van Loan soon began distributing dyes and manufacturing chemicals for other areas of the textile industry, including piece goods, upholstery, carpeting, and yarns, as well as offering products for other chemical companies.

Exceptional responsiveness to customer needs was high on the agenda from the beginning. In 1936 the company established an innovative customer service laboratory, one of the first in the South. Here precision color matching could be accomplished, processes tested, and manufacturing problems solved under conditions that duplicated those in the customers' plants.

Under the terms of the partnership agreement, ownership of the company passed to J. Wheeler Van Loan after Thomas Marlowe died in the 1960s. Still family-owned and operated, the company is in the hands of his children, Donald Van Loan, president, and Kathleen Van Loan Minchak, vice president. Approximately 40 people are employed at the High Point headquarters and at the distribution and sales facilities at Hickory Color and Chemical, a subsidiary in Hickory, North Carolina.

In 1990 Marlowe-Van Loan opened its new corporate offices and manufacturing plant on Ward Avenue. At the heart of this operation are two large state-of-the-art laboratories. The research and development laboratory conducts basic chemical research and chemical analysis and is responsible for product quality control. As a chemical company in the 1990s, its mission is to develop quality products that are both environmentally friendly and cost-effective for manufacturers. The 5,000-square-foot customer service laboratory is staffed with professionals who have over 100 years of combined hands-on mill

Marlowe-Van Loan's state-of-the-art customer service laboratory is staffed with professionals who have over 100 years of combined hands-on mill experience.

Donald Van Loan and Kathleen Van Loan Minchak, president and vice president, pictured here in the company's new corporate office in 1990.

experience, and is equipped with a computerized color-matching system.

Along with dyestuffs the company's product line includes scouring and leveling agents, dyeing assistants, lubricants, softeners, carriers, defoamers, fixatives, opticals, and many other specialty products. A major distributor of textile chemicals in the Southeast, Marlowe-Van Loan also has customers in Canada, Mexico, the Caribbean, and the Orient. A new market for the company has been an expansion into developing dyes used in furniture finishes.

While experiencing its own steady growth, Marlowe-Van Loan has contributed to the growth of its home community through support of many charitable organizations, the hospital, the arts, and numerous other civic endeavors. ❧

Max Meeks and Miss North Carolina take the platform at the dedication of the new Southern Furniture Exposition Building in the 1950s.

For more than 60 years, High Point's neighborly spirit has had a voice—radio station WMFR. Signing on in 1935, it was one of the first radio stations in the state. Like most pioneer stations, it filled the hours with local news and local musical talent. Stan Conrad and E. Z. Jones were the founders, and they sold the station to the Lambeth family about 1940.

Today WMFR is one of a family of four commonly owned radio stations which share engineering and broadcast facilities on N.C. Highway 68 South.

Max Meeks, WMFR's morning announcer for most of its history, began working at the station in 1947. After Naval service in World War II, he moved to High Point to attend High Point College. In his junior year he was asked by Frank Lambeth, who was the station manager for about 40 years, to fill in a summer vacancy. After a week he was hired permanently. Meeks loved the job from the first day, and has no thoughts of retiring.

Radio had played an important role, bringing people daily news of the war, but by the time Meeks arrived, people were predicting that television would be the death of the

older medium. Those forecasts proved to be wrong.

"Radio is as strong today as it has ever been," Meeks said. "It can do things that none of the other media can."

Meeks offered a few examples of the flexibility and immediacy of a local station. One morning the station got a call from a small store on Green Street. An elderly, disoriented woman wearing a nightgown had wandered into the store. All she could remember was her name. Meeks had the information on the air in three minutes. The woman's nephew heard it in his car and was at the store within 10 minutes.

On another occasion a local pastor called to say this son had lost his glasses while delivering

his newspaper route. A couple who had found the glasses on their morning walk heard the announcement, and the boy had them back by 8:30 A.M.

"These are simple things, but they are the things that make me enjoy it," Meeks said.

A popular feature has been the "Tell Your Neighbor" program, where callers exchange recipes, remedies, and household hints. WMFR-AM is all news and talk, 24 hours-a-day, and serves the High Point, Jamestown, Archdale, and Trinity communities. Listener participation is one of the keys to the strength of this format. WMFR has seven telephone lines to take calls from listeners.

WMFR's sister station, WMAG, was launched in 1983 and has always had an adult contemporary format. Bill Flynn, the popular *Morning Show* host, has been with the station from the beginning. The WMAG sound is familiar in offices around the Piedmont. Listeners spend their days with Lora Songster. Colin Garrett presides over afternoon drive time. WMAG serves a 14-county area that includes Guilford, Forsyth, Alamance, and Davidson.

WHSL, WHISTLE 100, began broadcasting "20 in a Row" country on September 22, 1995. In its first month on the air, the station played 10,000 songs in a row and awarded $20,000 cash to one lucky listener. The WHISTLE 100 day begins with *Mason*

The Happy Ramblers were part of the regular Saturday morning programming on WMFR in the mid-1940s.

Left to right: Max Meeks, Sportscaster Bill Smith; and Engineer Jack Boyd, broadcast live at a Golden Gloves Boxing Tournament held during the early 1950s at the High Point YMCA.

and Dixon in the Morning. Daytime announcers Jayme Austin and Rod Davis play "20 In a Row" country, including artists like Garth Brooks, Reba McEntire, and John Michael Montgomery.

The newest addition is WTCK-AM, the market's only sports talk station. THE TICK-ET was launched on March 4, 1996. The morning hosts, Matt and TJ, have captured attention with their topical and somewhat controversial brand of humor. Other members of the weekday lineup are John Renshaw, Kevin Wall, Papa Joe Chevalier, and Scott Ferrall. Along with sports talk, WTCK plans to provide play-by-play coverage of major sporting events, including the ACC Tournament, the Super Bowl, and the World Series. ∞

Max Meeks, WMFR's morning announcer since 1947, has no thoughts of retiring.

Leggett & Platt specializes in manufacturing and marketing components and related products for the home, office, and institutional furnishings industries and diversified markets. Among its products are bed frames and headboards, swivels, rockers and gliders for motion furniture, foam cushioning, and spring assemblies for beds and upholstered furniture.

Based in Carthage, Missouri, since it was founded in 1883 as an early manufacturer of coils for bedsprings, Leggett & Platt has had a High Point connection for some 20 years. In the 1970s, Leggett & Platt acquired a High Point manufacturing company, Carolina Spring.

Carolina Spring was established in 1936 by C. C. Edwards Sr., Clarence E. Lambeth,

and Frazer Edwards. For the first few years, the company operated from a brick building on East Broad Street. In 1939 Carolina Spring purchased a building at 101 West Point Avenue. It had originally been used for making railway cars, and later by a textile company. Carolina Spring added a story and remained at that location until 1968.

C. C. Edwards Sr., president of the company, was an educator who owned Edwards Business Colleges in High Point and Winston-Salem from 1909 until he sold the schools in the early 1930s. His son, C. C. Edwards Jr., joined the company in 1946 as secretary/treasurer. Clarence Lambeth was the plant manager. He had previous experience in spring manufacturing with the Nachman Corporation.

In 1968 Carolina Spring built a new facility on Sherman Road, which was later purchased by Leggett & Platt.

Leggett & Platt has been publicly traded since 1967, and was first listed on the New York Stock Exchange in 1979.

Carolina Spring, High Point, North Carolina, circa 1960s

Many companies pride themselves on their "family atmosphere," but few have more claim to being a family operation than Dallas Furniture. Many of its customers are the children and grandchildren of its first customers. And while the company has upgraded its merchandise, taken advantage of modern marketing techniques, and expanded its market to include all of the United States and beyond, employees enjoy the closeness and comraderie typically found in family relationships.

Sanders Dallas was the first president of the company, which came into being when Dallas, a manufacturer of living room furniture, bought Hendrix Furniture on December 31, 1937. Dallas and J. D. McCrery were two of the original four officers of the company.

McCrery vividly recalls three people who helped give the company its unique flavor and success—Dallas; Charles C. Hughes Sr., the first manager; and Carmen Criscoe, the premier salesman for 40 years.

"'Slim Dallas' was more expressive with his hands than anybody I ever saw," McCrery said. He was full of ideas, excited, and progressive. He was the first to have air-conditioned space at the furniture market. His creative displays dazzled buyers.

Dallas was quick to spot entrepreneurial opportunities. He bought an old house on Washington Street and sold used furniture from it. He bought rental property and ran the rental business from the Dallas Furniture store. Mr. Dallas retained ownership of his manufacturing company, Dallas, Inc., until 1961.

Charles C. Hughes was a wheeler-dealer, according to McCrery. "When he came out of the service, he would buy anything in the world. Once he bought a railroad car and rented it back to Southern Railroad."

Carmen Criscoe, who started working for Dallas Furniture in the 1940s, "sold more than anybody," McCrery said. Criscoe, now retired, was a born salesman who knew and remembered everybody, and is still a frequent visitor to the store.

In the late 1960s, Dallas Furniture attracted national media attention for its highly unusual sideline—arranging weddings. The company handled all the paperwork for couples; in the early years, couples were actually married in the store. Although this service is not advertised, over 3,000 couples have had their marriages arranged by Dallas Furniture.

Dallas Furniture occupied this site on Washington Street from 1939 to 1973.

In 1985 Sanders Dallas Jr., who became president of the company when his father retired, invited his wife, Vicki, to get involved in the business. Now vice president, she has played a major role in making Dallas Furniture what it is today—a home furnishings store with an inviting appearance and a strong commitment to customer service. Recently, two of the Dallas children have joined their mother in operating the store—John Sanders Dallas III, and Elizabeth Dallas Harrington. The staff, headed by manager Tamara Auman, is young and enthusiastic, and includes Christina Nicopolous Prentzas, assistant manager/sales; Wayne Lilly, sales; Kara Lane, property manager/sales; and Thomas McDonald and Glenn Williams, drivers.

Dallas Furniture is a source of quality furniture for customers everywhere. Out-of-state shoppers, catalog sales, and custom orders account for much of the business now, but the owners and employees are always happy to see the High Point area families they have served since 1937. ∾

The officers and employees of Dallas Furniture enjoy lasting friendships and a family atmosphere few companies can match. Pictured here are Sanders Dallas Jr., president, and J. D. "Mac" McCrery, secretary from 1937 to 1995.

Piedmont Chemical Industries

Over six decades, Piedmont Chemical Industries, Inc. has grown from a small manufacturer serving local textile companies to a company with four subsidiaries and customers in more than 30 countries worldwide. Its goal is to be the most self-sufficient supplier of textile chemicals in the world, while continuing to diversify into manufacturing chemicals for a broad array of other industries.

A close partnership with its customers has always been a hallmark of the company. Using the most advanced equipment, Piedmont Chemical helps customers solve chemical and processing problems that arise in their day-to-day operations. New products are tested in the laboratories on equipment that duplicates that of the customers.

Along with attentiveness to the changing needs of customers, Piedmont Chemical is alert to emerging markets, and committed to the extensive research and development needed for creating new solutions. Its history is a story of continuous innovation of processes, combined with a commitment to provide its customers with dependable quality and economy.

Piedmont Chemical's four manufacturing sites in three states together provide a complete line of chemicals used in processing textiles, producing over 70,000 metric tons of material annually. Each facility has its own research and development and quality control laboratories.

At the Ethox Chemicals, Inc. facility in Greenville, South Carolina, ethoxylated and propoxylated surfactants—the building blocks for many textile processing auxiliaries—are produced. These include detergents, lubricants, wetting agents, emulsifiers, and emollients. Ethox also makes products for the metalworking, paper, paint, personal care, mining, oil recovery, and agriculture industries.

Dooley Chemical Company, Inc. is in Chattanooga, Tennessee, a center of the carpet industry. It serves all major carpet manufacturers, and has developed new processing technology such as that used in producing stain-block carpeting. Dooley is also a major player in the finishing of fleece fabrics. Some six million pounds of fleece goods are napped every week using napping assistants produced by Dooley. Additionally, Dooley research and development has been responsible for breakthroughs in hosiery production.

Fibre Chemicals, Inc. in Anderson, South Carolina, was developed in partnership with leading synthetic fiber producers. At its state-of-the-art laboratories, such products as spin finishes, sewing thread lubricants, defoamers, oversprays, and special cleansers are manufactured, many of them custom-blended for particular customers.

At the headquarters facility in High Point, chemicals for all areas of textile wet processing are manufactured. The parent company, Piedmont Chemical Industries, also directs overall R & D and marketing strategies for the entire organization, under the leadership

Once the demand for synthetic fibers became strong in the late 1950s, Fred Wilson Sr. purchased a former trucking facility on High Point's Burton Street in which to manufacture textile chemicals for this growing market.

of Fred E. Wilson Jr.

Wilson said that his father, who died in 1985, would be amazed at the scope and sophistication of Piedmont Chemical Industries today. Fred Wilson Sr. launched the business in 1938, when he was 30 years old. He had been a successful salesman for a chemical company and thought he could do better on his own. Working from a small building on English Street, he mixed up the chemicals at night, sold them during the day, and sent out invoices on weekends.

After a struggle during the war years, when raw materials were difficult to obtain, Wilson saw his company begin to prosper when polyester and other synthetic fibers came into widespread use, bringing with them opportunities for new specialty chemicals. In 1957 the company bought an existing trucking facility on Burton Street, where the headquarters are still located. Over the years Piedmont Chemical bought all the adjoining properties, and the original building has been expanded several times.

Both of Wilson's sons grew up in the business, working in the plant during summer vacations, and assuming full-time positions after their graduations from college. Robert Wilson joined the company in 1954, and started his own business in a related industry during the 1960s. Fred Wilson Jr. came on board in 1961, and has headed the company since his father retired in the early 1980s.

As the domestic textile industry has matured, Piedmont Chemical has grown and thrived by diversifying into other industries and international markets. The company's products are used in everything from socks and seatbelts to skin softeners and spacecraft. It has ventured into relatively untapped markets in South America, Europe, and the Pacific Rim, often hand-in-hand with its customer companies.

Piedmont Chemical Industries' products have been to the moon—as lubricants in the insulation of nose cones and in astronauts' socks. They saw service in the Gulf War, incorporated into army camouflage uniforms.

Piedmont Chemical Industries, Inc. currently maintains its headquarters at the Burton Street location while the company has since expanded to include four subsidiaries serving customers in 30 countries.

And they've made thousands of appearances on national television, on the bodies of professional athletes. The uniforms used by the National Football League, among others, owe some of their wearability and washability to Piedmont Chemical.

One team even attempted to gain an advantage on the field through textile chemicals. Several years ago, an order from the Dallas Cowboys included a special request. The team wanted a double dose of silicone lubricant on its jerseys. The extra slick finish produced the desired effect—the players felt like greased pigs to anyone trying to tackle them. The situation came to the attention of then-Commissioner Pete Rozelle, who threatened to fine the Cowboys if they didn't shed their slippery gear.

Committed to innovation, customer service, and continued growth, Piedmont Chemical Industries also fully intends to remain a family-owned and operated company. Fred Wilson's two children, Fred E. "Rick" Wilson III and Creswell Wilson Davis, both followed their father's footsteps

in earning degrees in textile chemistry at North Carolina State University. Rick Wilson is vice president of sales; Cres Davis heads the human resources department. Both have young sons.

"We're here to stay," said Fred Wilson. "Three generations of the family have been active in the business, and the fourth is on the way." ∞

Wood-Armfield Furniture Company

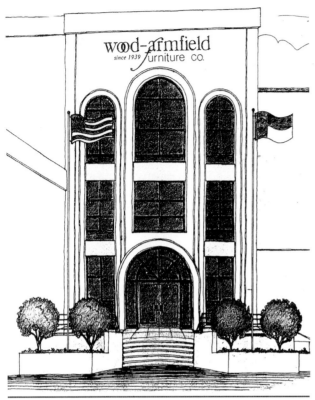

Wood-Armfield's present, 1996

In 1939 Carl Wood, a prominent local businessman, built a furniture and appliance store at 460 South Main Street. He was joined later in the business by Warren Armfield. All their customers were local, and linoleum, vacuum cleaners, and oil converters were their fast-selling items, along with furniture. The store was part of a three-building shopping strip, and as the business prospered, Wood-Armfield bought the small grocery and shoe storefronts to expand its store by 3,000 square feet.

Carl Wood retired in 1960, and Warren Armfield became the sole owner. He was joined later in that decade by his son, Jim.

In 1977 the business was purchased by Phil and Gloria Kennett, who had bought another furniture company, Utility Craft, two years earlier. Under the Kennetts' ownership, the store concentrated on higher-end furniture and accessories, a strategy that paid off in exceptional growth for its national and international business.

From a business with six employees and 10,000 square feet of space less than 20 years ago, Wood-Armfield has grown to a company with 175 employees and five locations—the Utility Craft, the expanded Wood-Armfield, showroom space in the Atrium, a service center, and a clearance store. The company maintains its own fleet of trucks for in-home deliveries east of the Mississippi.

Some 85 percent of Wood-Armfield's business is out of state, although the company does not advertise outside of North Carolina. Special orders account for about 80 percent. Kennett attributes the growth of national business to referrals from satisfied customers. North Carolina's lower prices bring people in, he said, but service is what keeps them coming back, and telling their neighbors, which expands the store's customer base.

It is not unusual for extended members of families and second generation members to buy from Wood-Armfield. The company is proud of the fact that 14 of their early

employees are still with the company after 10 years.

Helping people buy merchandise of their choice is the keystone of Wood-Armfield's growth. A large expert sales and design staff is divided into six units, each with its own office and support staff. An impressive work room filled with tables and chairs contains thousands of fabric swatches and product catalogs for customers to consider.

Consumers demand enormous choice today, and Wood-Armfield is staying abreast of that trend. A 1996 expansion has added another 102,000 square feet of showroom space, and connects the main store to its display space in the Atrium.

"A big furniture store in the 1980s had 30,000 square feet," Kennett said. "I never dreamed that we would need 160,000 square feet of display floor but Wood-Armfield wants to offer the customer the latest designs in furniture selection."

"We are looking forward to the future of Wood-Armfield and to that end have introduced our second generation of family into the business," Kennett concluded. ∽

Wood-Armfield's past, 1939

Morgan, Herring, Morgan, Green, Rosenblutt & Gill

"Now, what can I do to help you?" were the words most often on J. V. Morgan's lips. They represent the attitude of serving and caring that are carried on in the law firm he founded in 1942.

A High Point native, J. V. Morgan earned his law degree at the University of North Carolina at Chapel Hill. Soon after he established his general law practice, he built his own office on Commerce Avenue. After redevelopment projects took that block, he and others built the Law Building at 212 East Green Street in 1964. Always very active in civic work, Morgan is also remembered for his singing voice. Hundreds of High Point families asked him to sing at weddings and funerals, and he was a regular feature of Jaycee Jollies for 20 years.

Morgan's son, James F. "Jim" Morgan, joined the firm in 1970. The firm has five partners and one associate lawyer. Jim Morgan specializes in personal injury, probate, wills, and trials. He represented Guilford County in the North Carolina House of Representatives for three terms. Like his father, he is committed to giving back to the community, and has served as president or chairman of more than 40 organizations, including many High Point boards and the North Carolina Jaycees, the North Carolina Metropolitan Chambers of Commerce, and the United Way of North Carolina. He was twice named Young Man of the Year of High Point, and twice honored as one of the Five Outstanding Young Men in North Carolina. He is the 1996 president of the Guilford County Bar Association and chairman of the board of Guilford Technical Community College.

W. Dan Herring, a native of Rocky Mount, earned his law degree at Wake Forest University. His specialty practice areas are personal injury, family law, and civil litigation.

James M. Green Jr. was born in High Point and graduated from the Cumberland School of Law of Samford University. His practice areas include bankruptcy, civil litigation, personal injury, and criminal and domestic law.

David K. Rosenblutt is a native of New Jersey and a law graduate of Boston University. He specializes in litigation, bankruptcy, corporate law, probate, and personal injury.

James E. Gill Jr., was born in Detroit, grew up in High Point, and earned his law degree at Samford University. Gill specializes in trust, corporate law, real property, and probate.

Thomas W. Smothers joined the firm as an associate in 1995. A graduate of Campbell University School of Law, he appears in District and Superior Courts in civil and criminal cases, prepares briefs, motions, and pleadings, and conducts intake interviews. ∞

Founder J. V. Morgan (1918-82)

The Law Building of High Point

Paper towels, strapping, tape, fax, and copy paper—a full line of printing papers and hundreds of other products for industry are distributed by Henley Paper Company.

The business originated as Parker Paper and Twine, chartered in 1906 to serve the furniture industry in High Point. During the Great Depression, the company filed for Chapter 11 bankruptcy protection. Arthur B. "Shux" Henley, who was working for a paper company in Florida at the time, returned to his home state, bought the company, and brought it out of bankruptcy. It was reorganized as Parker Paper Company in 1934, and renamed Henley Paper Company 10 years later.

When Henley took over, the company was operating from a building on South Hamilton Street. As business improved, he bought the nearby Cox building, and those two buildings served as headquarters until 1975. The company had warehouse operations in Gastonia, and soon added warehouses and offices in Charlotte and Asheville. Before his death in 1979, Henley had added branches in Hickory, North Carolina, and in Greenville, South Carolina.

Henley was early to see that High Point, Greensboro, and Winston-Salem were developing into one market area, and he bought land for the new corporate headquarters right in the center of the Triad, off Sandy Ridge Road. The company moved into its new corporate offices on Triad Drive in October, 1975.

Henley had two sons, and Arthur Boyden Henley Jr. says his father had plans for their continuing the family business even before they could walk. Both brothers began with summer jobs at the company during their high school years. A. Boyden Henley Jr. is now president, and Nixon C. Henley (Nick) is executive vice president.

With this second generation, a branch has been opened in Raleigh, sales volume has doubled over a 16-year period, and Henley Paper Company employs some 300 people. Since 1984 it has been listed as one of the 100 largest privately owned companies in North Carolina. In its market area of North and South Carolina and parts of Georgia, Tennessee, Virginia, and West Virginia, the big Henley trucks are a common sight.

Henley Paper has long been a wholesaler of much more than paper and twine. Among the products it distributes are bobbins, pattern boards, and webbing for the furniture industry; washroom products; printing paper; and a vast array of packaging materials and machinery. Many of its suppliers are household names, including Weyerhaeuser, 3M, Scott Paper, Kimberly-Clark, and Solo Cup.

Brown kraft paper used to be a staple of the packaging industry, Boyden Henley says, but the increased use of plastic changed that. Now products are more likely to be shrink-wrapped, poly bagged, or encased in blister cards. Plastic strapping has replaced steel, and manufacturers protect the goods they ship with bubble wrap and foam peanuts instead of shredded or wadded paper.

But far from ushering in a paperless society, the Computer Age has witnessed an upsurge in the use of paper. Along with the thousands of reams of computer, copier, and fax paper it moves, Henley is a major distributor of coated and uncoated stock to printing companies. ∞

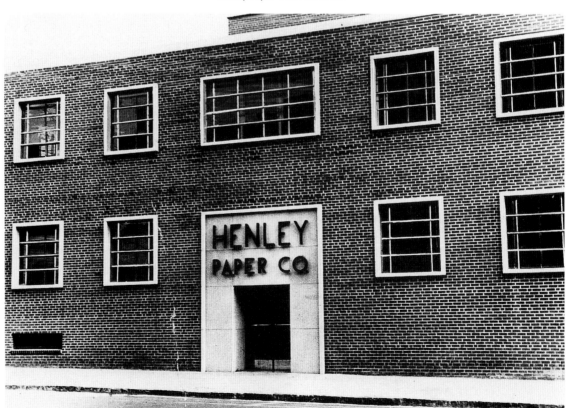

Henley Paper Co., circa 1950s

Left to right: John T. Davis Jr., president; Daniel K. Davis, vice president; Randall K. Davis, vice president

The Davis Furniture story reflects the spirit of enterprise so common in the development of the furniture industry in High Point. John Turner Davis Sr. brought his wife, Hattie Lee, to High Point in 1926, going to work for Tomlinson Furniture Company as an upholstery foreman.

In 1938 the Davises' oldest daughter, Dorothy, began as a bookkeeper with the new Heritage Furniture Company, where she eventually became an office manager. In 1940 John Davis Jr. joined his father as an employee at Tomlinson. With the onset of World War II, John Jr. joined the United States Coast Guard, seeing duty in the South Pacific.

John Davis recognized that with Dorothy's office experience and his furniture experience, they could start a company for themselves and reap more fully the benefits of their own labors. So in 1944 the family pur-

chased the small furniture repair business of Jasper B. Davis (no relation) at 1315 South Main Street, and the Davis Upholstery Company opened for business. John T. Davis and Dorothy L. Davis were listed as the proprietors, though Dorothy also continued to work at Heritage.

At first the focus of the business was repair work. Soon the Davis shop moved around the corner to 115 East Davis Avenue, at the south end of Hamilton Street. This early operation employed three upholsterers, a sewer, and a maintenance man, and had a finishing area on the second floor. Hattie helped out with the sewing when needed. Since the shop was next door to a city fire station, there was also a labor pool of off-duty firemen. After the war John Jr. married Frances Honbarrier, and joined the operation as a manager. By 1947 the company had added to its reupholstery work the manufacturing of occasional chairs, and eventually living room furniture.

In the early 1950s, reupholstery work became a thing of the past. The company listed as officers John T. Davis Sr., president; John T. Davis Jr., vice president of manufac-

turing; Hattie Davis, secretary; and Dorothy (Davis) Haines, treasurer. A parcel of land was acquired at 602 Linden (the company's current location), and a new building erected by 1953. Davis was finding a new market with colleges and universities up and down the east coast. When Florida State University placed an order for over 800 chairs in 1954, the firm had found its niche. For the next 25 years the emphasis would be on pieces for university environments.

Upon the death of his father in 1967, John T. Davis Jr. became president of Davis Furniture Industries, Incorporated. Through his leadership, both the product line and the physical plant were greatly expanded. During the 1970s, a new direction toward a complete range of office and executive furniture began to take shape, and both of John's sons joined the organization. Randall Davis, now executive vice president (of sales and marketing), joined the company in 1973, and Daniel Davis, the current vice president of manufacturing, in 1977. By the mid-1980s the institutional lines were replaced by licensing designs, primarily from Europe, to be manufactured in High Point for the contract office market.

Today, Davis Furniture is recognized as a leading manufacturer of contemporary office and executive furniture. Davis moves toward the twenty-first century committed to providing its employees with the best possible work environment and its customers with excellent value and superior quality. ∞

First advertisement from the 1945 High Point City Directory

Henredon Furniture Industries

Henredon was founded in 1945 by four men determined to build furniture of "custom quality." And today, fifty years later, among people of discriminating taste, the name Henredon represents the best America has to offer.

The initial product line consisting of just three chests has mushroomed into hundreds of beautiful wood and upholstery designs for every room. To the one original case goods facility in Morgantown, the company has added sizable manufacturing complexes in three other locations in North Carolina; and a workforce of 75 employees has grown to nearly 2,000.

Henredon's underlying philosophy has always been to make quality furniture for the middle- and upper-income end of the market, and it reaches these consumers by distributing through better department stores, design studios, and upscale furniture stores and by advertising in periodicals that cater to this clientele.

Folk wisdom in the furniture industry would have it that success depends upon product, people, and programs, and certainly Henredon has been blessed with all three.

For nearly 30 of its 50 years, Henredon's design direction was spearheaded by Ken Volz Sr. At the same time, the company has enlisted the talents of well-known creative artists in other fields—from Frank Lloyd Wright to Laura Ashley, Jack Lenor Larsen, Pierre Deux, Vincente Wolf, and, most recently, Ralph Lauren. In 1990 Henredon also became the furniture licensee for the prestigious Historic Natchez Foundation.

Of course, without talented leadership, success would not have been possible. And Henredon's unbroken chain has extended from its founders—T. Henry Wilson, Ralph Edwards, Donnell Van Noppen, and Sterling Collett—through Michael K. Dugan, who became Henredon's fifth chief executive officer on November 1, 1987.

In June of 1986 the Masco Corporation, a billion-dollar sales company headquartered in Taylor, Michigan, purchased Henredon and all its subsidiaries. And while a process of divestiture is now taking place, Henredon will remain what it has been for generations—one of the most respected and prosperous furniture companies in the industry, setting the standards for distinction of design, for quality of manufacture, and for the kind of pride and dedication to service that has been and will continue to be the major contributor to success. ☜

From an early age, the beauty of fine furniture inspired J. Dennis Young. His grandfather Ayers crafted a carved walnut bed that was given to Dennis's mother on her wedding day. Young was born in Stokes County, one of seven children. His father died when he was eight, and during the Depression he worked in the nearby textile mills, becoming an experienced knitter. His oldest brother, Bill Young, became Superintendent of Tomlinson Furniture Co. Seeing the well-crafted pieces the company turned out caused Dennis to decide that one day he too would go into the business.

Just before World War II he bought a half-interest in Quality Furniture Co. His partner was drafted right after the Pearl Harbor attack, and two years later Young also went into the service. He spent two years in the South Pacific aboard the Navy aircraft carrier *U.S.S. Hornet*, which was awarded 11 battle stars and a Presidential Citation. Young came through the war without a scratch, and working in the ship's supply store provided him with experience that would be useful when he started his own company.

The demand for furniture was great at the end of the war, but the supply was severely limited. Young worked, for a while, at a furniture store in Winston-Salem, and he recalls a day when eight mahogany bedroom suites came in. All were sold the same day, and one customer stayed until closing time, in the dwindling hope that one of the buyers might change his mind and free up a set of furniture.

In 1946 Young opened his own store in High Point, at 1706 North Main Street. (Becoming an entrepreneur enabled him to get some furniture for his own family—a local manufacturer advertised that it would sell two bedroom suites to any veteran who was starting his own company.) Young's started in 5,000 square feet of space, with two employees. The owner cheerfully worked six days and two nights a week to grow his business, and over the years bought the land adjacent to the store to enable its expansion to its current 50,000 square feet of beautiful display space.

Now in his 80s, Dennis Young is still active in the company. The business is run by his children, John D. Young, president, and Ann Young Upchurch, secretary/treasurer. This generation has built solidly on their father's commitment to carrying the best furniture and accessories, including many one-of-a-kind pieces. Their customers include royalty, celebrities, and many children of the store's original customers.

Loyal customers from all over the United States consider it worth the drive to find the right accessory, lamp, or sofa. New Yorkers have been known to say that it's easier to get to Young's than to the other side of Manhattan. Young's is also a favorite place of designers, who know it as a gold mine of unique, high-end items. Young's experienced design staff will always track down the particular look, the ideal piece a customer is trying to find.

The store that started when high quality furniture was scarce and hard to come by, now has the world from which to choose. Ann Young Upchurch literally shops the world for the distinctive pieces that give Young's a constantly changing, but always elegant, appearance. ∞

Dennis Young, pictured here the year construction began on Young's Furniture.

Allred Metal Stamping Works, Inc.

Raw material inventory as received for production

Members of the Allred family speculate that there are thousands, possibly millions, of households in America containing something made in their company plant on Old Thomasville Road. These products are invisible to consumers, however. They are the brackets and other small metal parts that are used in manufacturing furniture, cars, exercise equipment, toys, and tools.

The business was started in 1946 by A. L. Allred and Guy Brewer. Allred bought out Brewer's interest two years later, and the Allred family has owned and operated the company ever since. "A.L.," as he was affectionately called by his family and employees, continued to work every day until his sudden death in June, 1991, at age 86. The previous Christmas the employees had presented him with a plaque inscribed, "Thanks for being more than just a boss. We appreciate you."

The company's growth has been steady, and only once has it suffered a serious setback. On a July night in 1954, the Tate Building on West Greene Street, where Allred was then located, went up in flames. Two other commercial buildings in High Point burned the same night. The cause of the fires was never determined, but arson was suspected. Allred had only $18,000 in insurance coverage at the time. Some of the equipment was salvaged and rebuilt, and the company moved to new quarters at the intersection of Eastchester Drive and Centennial Avenue. Since 1964, Allred Metal Stamping has occupied its much larger facilities on Old Thomasville Road.

A. L. Allred's three sons, B.J., Carl, and Leonard, joined him in the business as soon as they were old enough, and with the exception of military service, have worked for the company all their adult lives. Mr. Allred's only daughter, Evelyn Allred Ward, has also worked for the company for many years. Five of the founder's grandchildren, Trina Allred Snider, Leigh Allred Mullinnix, Ray Allred, David Allred, and Wes Ward work in the family business, and the fourth generation is represented by Robert Snider.

In all, about 60 people work at the plant, many with more than 25 years' service. True to the company's family spirit, a big picnic was planned for the company's 50th anniversary celebration.

The company's building on Old Thomasville Road has been expanded nine times to accommodate the growing business. In 1994 Allred purchased 11 adjacent acres and an 80,000-square-foot building. About half of the orders now are from the furniture industry. Because of diversification, there are pieces from Allred Metal in locks, swing sets, garden tools, and sporting goods all across the United States. ∽

300-ton automatic punch press

In 1947 five Catholic Sisters arrived in High Point to establish a hospital. They were members of the Poor Servants of the Mother of God, an order founded by Fanny Taylor, a former volunteer nurse in the Crimean War under Florence Nightingale. While still in Crimea, Taylor was received into the Catholic Church. In England, she was joined by other young women who, in 1869, pledged themselves to lives of service to God and to the poor. Today, the Sisters of this order are trained nurses, teachers, and social workers; they live in England, Ireland, Scotland, Wales, Italy, France, Venezuela, Africa, and the United States.

The Sisters who came to High Point found that the community did not need another hospital, so they established a nursing home instead. They rented the Penny house at the corner of Penny and Greensboro Roads, and with help from the parishioners of Immaculate Heart of Mary Catholic Church and others, they equipped it to accommodate 22 residents. Word of the excellent care the Sisters provided soon spread. Before long, the Penny house was too small to hold all who wanted to come.

In 1950 the Sisters bought the house and 10 acres of surrounding land. Over the years they purchased additional land and received a donation of an adjoining 11 acres. The first expansion came in 1965, when a freestanding 60-bed nursing facility was completed with the help of private funds and the Medical Care Commission of North Carolina. In 1973 a 55-bed wing was added, with major donations from the Duke Endowment, Spencer-Love Foundation, and the Bryan Family Foundation. Maryfield Acres, a retirement community on the property, opened in 1979 and has grown to include 28 cottages.

Unlike many denominational nursing homes, Maryfield receives no subsidy from the Catholic Church. According to Sister Lucy Hennessy, administrator of the home, all hospitals, nursing homes, and schools operated by members of the Order must look to their own communities for support.

The people of High Point, and the surrounding region, have generously supported Maryfield throughout its history. Business people in the community have helped guide the Sisters since 1947, and in 1963 Maryfield's Advisory Council was formed. Business leaders were involved in planning and developing Maryfield Acres, and in 1981 they helped raise the money for an expansion that included an ecumenical chapel.

Since 1987, the board of directors has included lay leadership; and it was the board's decision in 1988 to launch a major renovation and expansion program. The Vision Campaign funds provided a new administrative wing, living room, solarium, dayroom, nursing station, and 17 private rooms. Maryfield also receives daily help from its volunteer group, the Blue Ladies, who assist with resident activities.

Donors, volunteers, residents, and staff come from every walk of life and all religious denominations. Says Sister Lucy, "I've never seen anything so ecumenical."

A not-for-profit, skilled, and intermediate care nursing home, distinguished for its compassionate care and home-like comfort, as well as its beautiful setting, Maryfield operates with a nonsectarian philosophy: "We

An aerial view of the convent and the present Maryfield Nursing Home and Retirement Center

believe that life is a gift from God. Each person's life is of great value and deserves respect and care in all its stages, from conception until death. It is our aim to provide skilled nursing care of the highest quality, based on sound medical principles, and to treat each individual with the respect and reverence fitting to his dignity as a human person." ∞

Left to right: Mrs. Melva Price, who welcomed the Sisters to High Point; Bishop Vincent Waters, who welcomed the Sisters to his diocese; Sr. Patrice, foundress of Maryfield.

"And the band played on." The Presbyterian Home Band has been a familiar friend to the people of High Point since its beginning in the middle 1960s. The rhythm band, made up of residents aged 69 to 96 playing homemade instruments, entertains at various functions in the Triad and across the state on an average of twice weekly. Photo by Donita Dunbar.

The Presbyterian Home of High Point opened in 1952, culminating eight years of planning which had begun in 1944 with a request from the Albemarle Presbytery to the Synod of North Carolina to investigate the advisability of establishing a home for the aged. The Reverend H. R. McFadyen and the Reverend R. Murphy Williams were instrumental in guiding the Home through incorporation in 1946. Twenty-seven and one-half acres of land on the original site of the George Penny Home were purchased in 1950 from High Point University. Built in 1922, a structure on the property, which had served as a Methodist orphanage and later as a men's dormitory, became the first Home and was dedicated on January 6, 1952.

By the end of its first year, the Presbyterian Home had 24 residents and 9 employees. Those residents who could afford to pay were charged $125 a month for their care, and the Home operated on an annual budget of approximately $57,500. Presently, the Presbyterian Home has some 300 residents, 210 employees, and an annual budget of just under $7 million. The difference between these statistics tells a story of changing attitudes about aging and lifestyle choices.

Today, the Home offers a full spectrum of services, from skilled nursing care to independent living. The largest and fastest growing group of people within the community are those seniors choosing independent living in apartments, cottages, and patio homes. The population is younger, healthier, and very active. Most are people who gladly trade the burdens of managing a home for the convenience of having their meals prepared or their groceries delivered, weekly maid service, an on-campus outpatient clinic, and a full array of social and recreational activities. The Home maintains its own 49-seat transit liner for excursions to Biltmore House, the Outer Banks, Charleston, and other points of interest, as well as outings to local cultural events. For the residents, it is a real home, to which they are happy to invite their families and friends for celebrations such as the annual Christmas buffet or a gala Mother's Day luncheon.

Very much a part of High Point community life, the Home is highly visible in the region through its traveling rhythm band. The Presbyterian Home Band, which began in the early days, plays on homemade instruments and performs an average of two engagements a week for church, civic clubs, and other organizations in the area.

Through growth and change, The Presbyterian Home of High Point has maintained its focus on care and concern for quality of life. The Home is a leader in recognizing and responding to trends in its field, and is proud to bear the seal of the Accreditation Commission of the American Association of Homes and Services for the Aging (AAHSA). From the beginning, there has been a priority to constantly strive to maintain quality of service, and assure those who have chosen the Presbyterian Home as their home of its position as one of the area's top retirement facilities now and into the twenty-first century. ∞

Some things never change! This sign on the Greensboro Road side of the Presbyterian Home of High Point is virtually the same today as it was in 1952 when the Home opened. The original building, built in 1922, was demolished in November of 1986 to make way for the modern six-story structure that many of today's residents call home.

High Point Sprinkler Company, Inc.

An airplane hangar in Washington, D.C., gets fitted with a system from High Point Sprinkler Company.

What do the Atomic Energy Commission, the National Gallery of Art, the Pentagon, the Greensboro Coliseum, North Carolina Memorial Hospital, and oil rigs off the Gulf of Mexico have in common?

They all have fire protection systems designed and installed by High Point Sprinkler Company. This High Point company has installed automatic sprinkler systems for customers in many parts of the world, including recent projects in the Caribbean, Sudan, and Guantanamo Bay, Cuba.

The company was started by three local businessmen in 1952, when newly revised building codes in the United States created a demand for more fire protection systems. The growth of the company is associated with the Aldridge family, beginning in 1954 when William F. "Bill" Aldridge was hired as sales manager. Bill Aldridge was appointed general manager three years later and president in 1967. By the mid-1970s he had acquired ownership of the company. His son, H. B. "Sonny" Aldridge, was elected president

in the early 1980s, and purchased the company upon his father's retirement in 1986.

The first sprinkler system was a grid of wooden pipes devised in the late 1800s by a New England textile manufacturer to protect his mill. From that first experiment to the present day, building codes, construction methods, and design technology have undergone enormous changes. What has not changed is that there are still no fire protection engineering programs in technical schools and universities. All the training and development comes from within the construction industry itself.

For most of their relatively short history, sprinkler systems have been designed to protect property. Even in modern "fireproof" construction, where walls and floors are not flammable, sprinklers are installed to protect property, furnishings, and other contents of buildings. A recent trend, said Sonny Aldridge, is to install sprinklers in residential buildings, to protect life. As municipalities grow, they look for alternatives to the expense of building additional fire stations. More of High Point Sprinkler's business now is with condominium and apartment complexes. These new, highly effective sprinkler systems detect fire in its earliest stages and sound an alarm. No multiple deaths from fire have ever been reported in buildings equipped with sprinklers. Retrofitting old buildings with modern sprinkler systems has become a major portion of the company's business.

The advances in fire protection technology can be seen in High Point Sprinkler's changes of address. Their first home was a small building on Virginia Avenue. In 1960 the company moved to big-

ger quarters on U.S. Highway 29-70, with more space for fabrication and offices to accommodate the growing design staff and their large drafting tables. In 1996, with about 60 employees, the company built a new 50,000-square-foot office and fabrication facility. The drafting tables have given way to computers, and design of all systems is computer-assisted. The four types of sprinklers in use when Sonny Aldridge joined the company in 1970 had grown to 75 types by 1996, with new materials and improved methods of joining pipes.

Throughout its history High Point Sprinkler Company has been an industry leader and a partner in the growth of its home community. Bill Aldridge was instrumental in forming the Southeastern Sprinkler Association and was active in the National Fire Protection Association. Sonny Aldridge is president of the Carolinas chapter of the American Fire Sprinkler Association. The company and its employees support the communities of High Point, Thomasville, and Archdale through participation in school programs, High Point Regional Hospital, High Point University, the YMCA, Boys and Girls Clubs, and several civic organizations. ☞

This circa 1960s photograph shows a portable sprinkler system created by High Point Sprinkler Company to demonstrate to firemen how its systems work.

In the early 1950s, when thousands of Americans were bringing home their first television sets, the big question was, "Where are we going to put the it?" Felix F. Miller Sr., the owner of retail appliance stores in High Point and Winston-Salem, came up with an answer. After work at night, he and his son, Felix Miller Jr., began building simple wood tables, just the right size and height to hold an early model TV.

The demand was so great that Miller sold his stores and began making tables full-time in 1954, calling his new venture Miller TV Products. Before long, the manufacturers of television sets, all U.S. companies, recognized the potential of TVs as furniture. RCA and others contracted with Miller to build television cabinets in the sophisticated Early American, French Provincial, and Contemporary styles that were popular at the time.

Miller TV Products was one of 11 companies around the country whose entire business consisted of producing cabinets as subcontractors for television manufacturers. Meeting the demands of the manufacturers was a frustrating and difficult business because their ironclad specifications led to inefficiencies and high costs.

Nevertheless, Miller devised a way of cutting down production, shipping, and warehousing costs. The company began shipping finished components, which could easily be assembled in the manufacturers' plants. A box of a size to hold one fully assembled TV cabinet could contain the components of half a dozen cabinets.

Knock Down (KD) furniture, as it was called, represented a major departure from traditional manufacturing processes, and Miller was the first to make TV cabinets that way. The usual method was to cut the components, sand and plane them so they would fit together smoothly, and then apply finishes to the whole piece. So much handwork was involved in the fitting and assembly that each article was virtually customized.

The furniture industry as a whole was wedded to this process because of the nature of the raw material. Wood contracts and expands with variations in temperature and humidity. It seemed inevitable that shaping and smoothing and adjusting were necessary to work the living material into finished furniture.

Felix Miller Jr. figured differently. He saw that the solution was controlling the moisture content of the wood, then cutting and boring the components to very strict tolerances. He was inspired in part by the metal industry, which had long been assembling products from pre-finished components.

Miller was ahead of his time, and his experience in component parts-based furniture placed the company in good stead when it was time to diversify. By 1970 there were too many problems associated with being a subcontractor only—RCA, General Electric, and the other television manufacturers became more interested in plastics and other low-cost materials than in wood, and they were setting up their own shops for cabinet building. Miller decided to branch into office furniture, and in 1971 the company began making desks at night, after the cabinet-making shift was over. By mid-1972 the company was making office furniture exclusively.

A satisfying footnote to the company's early history is that in 1978, General Electric, having failed to produce the high-quality wood TV cabinets for which there was a strong and growing demand, came back and

asked Miller TV Products to handle that part of their business. Of the eleven companies that had once made wood cabinets, nine had gone out of business. The offer was flattering, and the terms were very attractive, but Felix Miller Jr. declined. "I made my last TV cabinet in 1972," he told them.

Miller TV Products has been known as Miller Desk, Inc. since 1974. The company's executive management positions are held by Felix Miller Jr. and his five sons as follows: Felix Miller Jr.—chairman; Felix "Phil" Miller III—president; Max Miller—executive vice president/National Sales; David Miller—senior vice president/Purchasing; John Miller—senior vice president/Regional Sales; and Bobby Miller—executive vice president/Manufacturing. Mr. Miller's youngest child, Molly, is a member of the board of directors.

Company headquarters are at the same location where Felix Miller Sr. turned out his TV tables, at the corner of Ward and Lincoln Streets. Like most furniture companies in High Point, it has been expanded many times over the years.

From one plant with 180 employees, Miller Desk has grown to a company with five plants and 600 people. Two case-good plants and one seating plant are located in High Point. The company's two dimension lumber mills in Elkins, West Virginia, process rough-cut boards into component furniture parts. Miller Desk uses the majority of these products; the excess is sold to other manufacturers.

Aggressive marketing and merchandising programs have always been part of the corporate philosophy. In a highly competitive industry, Miller Desk thrives by meeting consumer demands for choice, quality, and quick availability. In the Miller Office Seating division, for example, over 500 basic styles of chairs are offered in thousands of combinations of wood, finish, and fabric colors. Any chair can be shipped in three weeks or less.

Over the years, Miller Desk has continued to use the time-proven construction techniques it used to make TV cabinets—solid hardwood parts, zero-tolerance mortise and tenon joints, and boxed-end dovetailed drawers. Building in this kind of quality pays off in an excellent reputation and strong sales, because office furniture has to stand up to hard use. In the 1990s, the company's market has grown to include customers who might be said to have paid too much or too little in earlier office furniture purchases. The former have learned to recognize value; the latter, to appreciate quality.

Once considered basically utilitarian, office furniture has changed dramatically.

Business people now look not only for durability and function, but also for a stylish image, fashionable colors and fabrics, comfort, and ease. Other trends that contribute to a growing market for Miller Desk and account for expansion of the product line are the popularity of home offices, the computerization of all offices, and the demand for ergonomically designed seating. Along with a tremendous variety of desks and chairs, Miller Desk makes computer stations, conference and occasional tables, executive office furniture, bookcases, storage cabinets, and file cabinets.

Miller Desk is a strong community supporter with a particular emphasis on contributing to programs that provide opportunities for underprivileged youth. ☜

Left to right: Founder Felix Miller Sr. and Chairman Felix Miller Jr., in office of the original retail appliance store

The Hi-Toms (High Point-Thomasville) minor league baseball team was a popular fixture in the 1950s. *Left to right*: Paul Byers, Jim Herndon, Maurice Wimbrow, and Vincent Pizzitola. *Photo courtesy The High Point Museum Archives.*

GTCC's mission is to prepare people for the workforce. In 1993 GTCC identified workforce preparedness as the top issue facing the college and the county. A 1995 survey of employers and employees identified skills the workers of the twenty-first century will have to have: teamwork, problem solving, listening, responsibility, and ethics. Educational institutions must do a better job of graduating students who have those skills. GTCC has joined with civic, education, and business leaders in Guilford County to find ways to integrate academic and technical teaching and learning and to use work-based learning opportunities to prepare students to be productive workers.

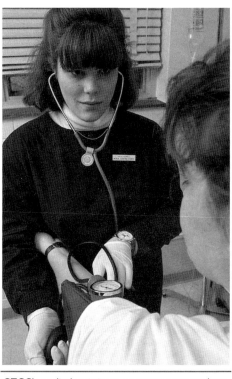

GTCC's medical assisting program prepares students to work in a health care setting doing tasks from scheduling appointments to drawing blood for testing. Medical assisting is one of several health care programs offered at the college.

Training Guilford County's workforce has always been the primary purpose of Guilford Technical Community College, which opened as Guilford Industrial Education Center in 1958. A collaborative venture between the State Department of Trade and Industrial Education and the school systems of Guilford County, High Point, and Greensboro, the school opened in the old Guilford County Tuberculosis Sanatorium in Jamestown. After adding a college transfer program in 1983, the school changed its name from Guilford Technical Institute to Guilford Technical Community College.

From an initial enrollment of 50 and a curriculum of two courses, GTCC has grown to serve more than 30,000 people each year through 60 certificate, diploma, and degree programs and numerous continuing education programs.

The college's main campus is in Jamestown, where the sanatorium's gazebo still stands, a reminder that GTCC is the gateway to success for its students.

GTCC also has campuses in High Point and Greensboro that make the college accessible to most people in the county.

The High Point campus is home to an upholstery program and a new drug and alcohol technology program that prepares people to work as substance abuse counselors. The High Point campus also offers adult basic education, adult high school, GED preparation, and continuing education courses ranging from computer classes and teacher recertification to arts and crafts, foreign languages, and human relations.

One of GTCC's best-known services is employee training. Economic developers regard GTCC as one of their primary assets in recruiting new industry to Guilford County. The college's Business and Industry Services division assists businesses in every training need, from revamping management styles to teaching production techniques. The full-time faculty in this division all have industry experience in fields ranging from furniture and textiles to sales and management.

The strength of the Business and Industry division is its ability to customize any program to a business's needs and to teach classes on a GTCC campus or at a business site.

GTCC is committed to meeting the needs of the people of Guilford County for skills training and the needs of the county's businesses for well-trained employees. The college's partnerships with business and industry are resulting in stronger programs, access to more up-to-date equipment, and, ultimately, better-prepared students. ∽

GTCC's High Point campus, in the heart of the nation's furniture capital, is home to the college's upholstering program. Students learn the fundamentals of working with wood frames, developing patterns, and industrial cutting and sewing.

One day in 1958, Walt Blackburn dropped by to visit his father-in-law, Lester P. Adams. The older man was in his backyard, running a string around four sticks he had stuck in the ground.

"I'm going to build me a hobby shop," Adams explained. Blackburn picked up a shovel and started digging the foundation Adams had marked out.

Adams was an experienced craftsman, having worked for Tomlinson Furniture, and his idea was to make wood turnings in his new 20' x 20' hobby shop. Blackburn began spending his afternoons and evenings working in the hobby shop, after he'd finished driving his delivery route for a bread company. After two and a half years, he joined the company full time, although it seemed a risky step for a young man with family responsibilities.

"It started with nothing but an idea," Blackburn said. Adams persuaded his wife to become an investor. She lent him $2,400 of her earnings from her home beauty shop, and he fretted about paying her back.

"It's bad enough to work with creditors all day, Adams used to say, and then you have to sleep with them at night," Blackburn recalls.

More than a dozen turning companies were operating in the area, and the competition was stiff. Still there was a considerable market in the 1960s for table legs and parts of etageres, and business was good. The company soon underwent a 50-percent expansion—10 more feet were added to the hobby shop. Before long, a second building was needed for storing materials. The company rented a small building on Woodbine Street, which was then a dirt road. Over the years Adams Wood Turning purchased that lot and the adjoining properties as they became available. When it had acquired more than 51 percent of the total street frontage, the company helped pay to have Woodbine paved. From the original 400-square foot backyard operation, the company has grown in size to over 50,000 square feet at its Woodbine Street location.

By 1966 Blackburn was seeing limitations to the wood turning business, and wanted to diversify into something that would not compete with the company's customers, but would make use of its existing equipment. He decided on lamps.

Adams Wood Turning took its first few lamps, under the name of Woodcraft Originals, to the fall furniture market in 1969.

"After four days of showing, we had $2,200 in orders," Blackburn said. "But that was $2,200 more than we had the year before."

In the following years, the company grew to be a major producer of lamps, made not only of wood, but also of brass, porcelain, crystal, and hand-thrown pottery. The Sedgefield by Adams line of classically styled and quality manufactured lamps had over 500 skus in 1996, and had become a household word with consumers. Through licensing agreements, certain models are also sold as part of designer groups, including the Bob Timberlake Collection, Norman Rockwell, and New Orleans Collections.

The strategy all along has been to sell to independent retailers, so as not to be dependent on any one customer. Wood turning remains a thriving part of the business, where turnings from bedposts to bunn feet are produced for furniture and upholstery companies without turning capabilities.

All three of Blackburn's children, Terri Thomas, Sherri Mickey, and Keith Blackburn, work in the family-owned business. Of the approximately 60 employees, many have been with the company since its earliest years, and many enjoy it so much that they never want to retire. At Adams Wood Turning they don't have to—in 1996 the oldest employee was 82. ∞

The idea for Adams Wood Turning began in 1958 in this hobby shop owned by Lester P. Adams.

raging nor'easter off Cape Hatteras on a May morning in 1959 set in motion a string of ideas that came to be realized as Hatteras Yachts, the world's leading manufacturer of luxury yachts. That morning, Willis Slane, a High Point hosiery manufacturer and avid sportsfisherman, was grounded. The wooden boats he and his friends owned were no match for the rough seas at Cape Hatteras, graveyard of the Atlantic.

As the wind howled, Slane told his fishing buddies that someday someone would build a boat that could withstand stormy weather, and it would probably be made of fiberglass. Ideally, the boat would be 40 feet long, he mused, big enough to accommodate a party of four with a salon, staterooms, and a complete galley. Such a boat, Slane believed, could even be built in High Point, the national capital of the wood furnishing industry.

His cronies thought he was crazy. Fiberglass was for bathtubs, they told him, and High Point was a good 200 miles from the ocean. But the idea stayed with Slane, and he soon persuaded 20 of his friends to put up the capital to start a company. In a rented garage on Wrenn Street, Slane embarked on an exhaustive study of the yacht market and mapped out in his mind the boat he wanted built. He then engaged a young naval architect, Jack Hargrave, and assembled a production crew.

Hatteras builds over 20 models of luxury motor yachts and sportfishing convertibles from 39 feet to 130 feet, including the Hatteras 54 Convertible (pictured above).

What came out of the garage four months later was a 41-foot boat, the largest craft ever constructed of fiberglass. She was hauled to Morehead City for launching. On March 22, 1960, Slane's wife, Doris, broke the traditional bottle of champagne across her bow, christening her *Knit Wits*—a fitting name for a vessel financed largely by a group of textile executives.

From that first history-making model, Hatteras Yachts has grown to a company that produces fishing boats and cruising yachts from 39 feet to 130 feet in length. The *Knit Wits* proved that fiberglass was the way of the future, and revolutionized the yacht-building industry.

Since 1969, Hatteras Yachts has also been building boats at its New Bern plant, located at the mouth of the Neuse River. The New Bern facility was opened to build vessels that are too large to be trucked down the highway. The manufacturing space itself is enormous, bigger than 10 football fields. In 1996, Hatteras employs over 1,100 people in its two locations.

The company produces more than 20 models of yachts, of which the largest belong to its Custom Yacht Series, introduced in 1989. Customers work closely with teams of highly experienced architects, engineers, designers, builders, and decorators in the creation of their "dream boats," which may cost up to $9 million. "Owner input" has always been encouraged by the company, and many options are available on every Hatteras model.

Fiberglass is the material that has enabled Hatteras to make ever-larger boats, but an insistence on quality is what has made it the world leader. From the start, the company has placed great emphasis on research, testing, and quality control. Almost every component, from fuel tanks to propeller shafts to stateroom mattresses, is produced in-house. Hatteras uses advanced CAD-CAM engineering technology to build yachts that maximize space while maintaining the style and beauty that have become synonymous with the Hatteras name.

Since 1985, Hatteras Yachts has been a division of Genmar Industries, Inc., the world's largest privately-held boat company.

Company founder, Willis Slane—High Point textile executive and ardent fisherman—stands in front of the 41-foot *Knit Wits*, the first boat over 30 feet to be built of fiberglass.

High Point is home to a television station that can make some impressive claims. WGHP has the largest news-gathering staff of any broadcast facility serving the market. The station does more local news than any station in town. And the station is owned by Rupert Murdoch, one of the biggest media moguls in the business.

Despite its size, the FOX 8 news team is very down-to-earth. Whether it's a story about a unique individual featured as one of Roy's Folks or a story solving a problem of a High Point neighbor in a Contact 8 segment, FOX 8 reflects our community. Since 1963 the station has been involved in covering the people, issues, and concerns of our town. But there have been some changes along the way.

From 1963 to 1995, WGHP was an ABC affiliate. Then on the very day the Carolina Panthers played their first NFL game, WGHP became a FOX affiliate. In fact, the game was the station's first broadcast with the new network, and the opportunity to air the Panthers games was one of the main reasons WGHP elected to join FOX.

The other reason stemmed from the fact that the affiliation enabled FOX 8 to broadcast local news at 10 each night. People wake up early in the Furniture City, and FOX 8 offered the market's only "news before you snooze."

FOX is the fastest growing network, and it's part of one of the fastest growing media companies, News Corp. WGHP is one of the 22 stations owned by the company and is one of over 200 affiliates. Rupert Murdoch has built a company based on media synergy. News Corp. owns Twentieth Century Fox

Carol Andrews and Fred Blackman of FOX 8 News

movie studios, Twentieth Century Television Productions, *TV Guide*, the *London Times*, the *New York Post*, and satellite companies all over the world.

A key to FOX's strategy is major sporting events. The company surprised the sporting community and CBS by securing the rights to the National Football League in 1994. FOX added the National Hockey League in 1995 and then Major League Baseball in 1996.

FOX 8 is involved in our community. At Christmas, the station hosts two free holiday concerts with the Winston-Salem and Greensboro Symphonies. Families attending bring cans of food that are used during the year by the area Salvation Army units. In 1995, 65,000 cans of food were collected, making the FOX 8 concerts the largest food

drive in the Piedmont. Also, the station conducts the biggest new toy drive in the area in an effort called Gifts for Cynthia's Kids. This important campaign provides a happy Christmas morning to more than 4,000 local foster children. The station is also dedicated to cleaning up area waterways in The Big Sweep, and regularly works with the events of Brenner Children's Hospital.

The station provides free air time to non-profit efforts in High Point. It focuses on the challenges and successes off our town in its news coverage. All in all, High Point can be proud of its hometown station, FOX 8. ∞

Left to right: Van Denton, Neill McNeill, Cynthia Smoot, and Rich Brenner of FOX 8 News

This Liberty Bell replica was one of several which toured the country. Horace Haworth, Sr., is reading a proclamation; High Point Mayor Bill Bailey is to his right; WMFR radio personality Max Meeks is holding the microphone to his left. Location: Main Street bridge. *Photo courtesy The High Point Museum Archives.*

High Point National Furniture Mart

High Point National Furniture Mart, a nine-story landmark in downtown High Point

The High Point National Furniture Mart is one of the many buildings in the city that is open for business just 18 days a year, during the spring and fall furniture markets. The nine-story landmark at the corner of Main and Commerce Streets is the showcase for 55 furniture companies.

This "shopping center" has grown along with the growth of High Point as the furniture market capital of the world.

It began with eight floors of showroom space, developed by J. L. Fine, and first opened for the 1964 fall market. The Fine family added 80,000 square feet in 1969, 20,000 in 1976, and 60,000 in 1978. Under new ownership in 1987, a final addition of 12,000 square feet was completed.

The High Point Furniture Mart is now owned and managed by the Berkshire Group, a national real estate financial services firm with headquarters in Boston, Massachusetts. In 1993 a $2.5-million renovation of the High Point Furniture Mart's interior began. Over a four-year period all the interior corridors have been widened, and the showroom space has been reconfigured to conform to tenants' needs and current interior design trends.

Ivan Garry presides over the Furniture Mart as general manager. He works on his tenants' behalf all year round, and is their genial host at market time. Garry has been with the High Point Furniture Mart since 1976. His face is a familiar one in downtown High Point, as is that of the Mart's long-time director of admissions, Lettie Owens, and loading-dock foreman, Clemon Walls.

Garry and his staff have as their mission statement "To provide a safe, friendly, clean and modern showroom facility in which to do business in a hassle-free environment during the Market." ∞

The friendly, familiar faces of High Point National Furniture Mart's staff

Reflections of the Past

High Point's past and present meet at The High Point Museum as it vibrantly fulfills its mission of encouraging a sense of heritage, place, and community.

Like many American cities, High Point began to get serious about preserving its past in the 1960s. In 1963 the Chamber of Commerce formed a committee to investigate the idea of starting a museum. That group developed into the Greater High Point Civic Center and Museum Corporation in 1964 with plans to develop a civic center/convention hall/museum complex on an entire block in the downtown area. When that project did not materialize, the City of High Point's Historical Commission adopted the dream of constructing a city museum. Meanwhile, artifacts and other historical memorabilia were stored and exhibited in the Little Red Schoolhouse, a building that had been used as an educational annex from 1931 to 1961. Though it was a much-beloved structure, the Little Red Schoolhouse did not have adequate storage, and the Historical Commission knew that it needed to consider other options for The High Point Museum's growing collection.

The year 1966 proved to be a watershed with three events that propelled the city closer to its goal of having a new museum facility. First, a January announcement of extensive roadwork which would cut through the Little Red Schoolhouse property forced the Historical Commission to find a new location for the Museum. Then, in order to preserve High Point's oldest house on its original foundation and to give the citizens a "historical park," the Historical Commission bought the historic Haley's Inn property from Capus Waynick in September. Simultaneously, the Historical Commission helped form a private, not-for-profit organi-

zation called the High Point Historical Society, which incorporated in December.

The High Point Historical Society immediately launched a $250,000 building fund campaign for a 14,000-square-foot museum to be located adjacent to Haley's Inn (now known as the Haley House) on East Lexington Avenue. Construction began in 1969, and a "new" High Point Museum opened to the public in October 1971. The Little Red Schoolhouse was moved from Ray Street to one-half block from the Museum in 1987; it is now used for public programs.

While the Museum was being constructed, the Historical Society concentrated its efforts on completing the restoration of the Haley

Costumed guides bring High Point's colonial heritage to life in the High Point Museum's Historical Park and showcase some of the Museum's finest artifacts.

House and on creating a "historical park" on the surrounding grounds. The City of High Point and the Historical Society then forged an agreement that is still operable today— the City of High Point owns and maintains all buildings and properties while the Historical Society operates the Museum and Historical Park as well as administers three off-site historic properties (Little Red Schoolhouse, Mendenhall Store, Jamestown Meeting House).

In its exhibits and programs, the Museum consciously illuminates the present through connections with the past. Its permanent collection includes textiles, tools, furniture, toys, early telephone equipment, architectural artifacts, as well as documents and photographs of earlier life in the High Point area.

Local residents are encouraged to share their artifacts and their memories. This philosophy creates close ties between

The John Haley House, built in 1786 according to Quaker Plan, is the centerpiece of the Historical Park. *Photos by Richard Haggerty for The High Point Museum & Historical Park.*

the Museum and the community, helps shape exhibit themes, and promotes greater involvement in Museum activities. The ever-changing exhibit schedule also stimulates thought and discussion about current issues and events.

The Museum regularly offers educational programs that correlate with its exhibits and with the city's heritage. The Second Tuesday Series offers a veritable smorgasbord of cultural opportunities with its monthly lectures, panel discussions, performances, and/or demonstrations. Annual activities include festivals, trips, classes, history camps, and July 4th and holiday celebrations.

A short stroll from the Museum, visitors are transported through two centuries of history as they enter the two and one-half acre Historical Park. The Haley House anchors the park with its status as a National Historic Site. John and Phebe Haley built their home in 1786 on what was then the main trade route between Petersburg, Virginia, and Salisbury, North Carolina. A blacksmith by trade, John Haley was also active in civic life, receiving Guilford County appointments as tax assessor, sheriff, and road commissioner. Improvements to the road system led to the establishment of several inns along that stage route, which in turn prompted the development of the surrounding Piedmont wilderness. Ironically, after Haley's death, his home was used as an inn during most of the 1800s.

Two other structures were brought to the Historical Park and restored in the early 1970s. Moved from its original 1750s site in nearby Davidson County, the Blacksmith

Renowned architect and painter Louis Voorhees designed the Little Red Schoolhouse, used to house overflow students from Ray Street Elementary School, 1931-61. His wife, Elizabeth Peyton Voorhees, served as its first teacher.

Hear the clanging of hammers and feel the heat from the red-hot coals as the blacksmith demonstrates his craft on weekends. *Photos by Richard Haggerty for The High Point Museum & Historical Park.*

Shop, outfitted with a working forge, opened in 1972. A 1770s log cabin built by Quaker potter Phillip Hoggatt was moved in 1973 to the park from its original site off Rotary Drive in High Point. Today, both structures are used for demonstrations of colonial crafts such as blacksmithing and weaving.

On weekends, costumed guides conduct tours of all three Historical Park buildings. With advance reservations, visitors may tour the buildings during the week. On designated weekends each year, the Guilford Militia Living Historians encamp in the Historical

Park, bringing the sights and sounds of eighteenth-century colonial life to the present with domestic skills and medical demonstrations, live musket and rifle firings, and period military drills.

The City of High Point provides approximately 60 percent of The High Point Museum and Historical Park's annual operating costs. The remaining 40 percent comes from individual donations, from memberships, and from corporate and foundation grants.

In 1996 The High Point Museum and Historical Park launched a $2-million capital campaign to expand and renovate its facilities and its educational programs for the benefit of High Point's residents and visitors. The expansion includes a new facade, a two-story addition, as well as a new lobby and store; renovation plans will make more efficient use of the current gallery and office spaces. The new addition will house an educational/meeting area equipped with high-tech audiovisual capabilities and theater-style seating for up to 220 people; new exhibit galleries; and a state-of-the-art storage facility, complete with a conservation laboratory, for the Museum's collections.

As the new millennium approaches, The High Point Museum and Historical Park continues to celebrate the families and the industries which have created High Point's prosperity and quality of life, and to embrace the fresh, exhilarating "history" of its present and future. ∞

First Factors Corporation

When Earl N. "Phil" Phillips Jr., James E. Foscue, and W. M. Webster established First Factors Corporation in 1972, they were offering a service to manufacturing companies that goes back to colonial times.

The first factors were agents for eighteenth-century British merchants, who provided them with assurance that the goods they sold in America would be paid for. In the early part of the twentieth century, when textile and furniture companies were established in the High Point area, factoring companies were often an essential ingredient in their success. By turning over their accounts receivable to a factor, fast-growing and often undercapitalized manufacturing companies could be assured of healthy cash flow and credit protection.

Phillips, Foscue, and Webster all had experience in the factoring business when they formed First Factors. They also had family and friends in the local furniture and textile companies which relied on factors as partners in their growth. The firm opened for business in a warehouse building on South Main and, needing more space, moved to its present central downtown location in the former First Citizens Bank building before 1980.

By 1990 First Factors had bought the building, and its name in bold letters across the top became a center city signpost. By then, also, First Factors had expanded well beyond the local market, to become the largest independent factoring company in the United States, and perhaps the world.

Initially serving just the region, the company has grown through acquisitions as well as internally created start-up divisions and joint ventures to exploit specialty financing niches. Colonial Acceptance Corporation in Mount Holly, North Carolina, was acquired out of bankruptcy in 1984. Ten years later, Southeastern Factors was organized to offer factoring services to start-up and early stage companies. This division, in turn, has co-ventured with various strategic partners to set up a U.S. Government accounts receivable financing unit and to establish High Point Capital, a business providing secured, short-term bridge financing coupled with ownership opportunities.

In the 1990s, the world is First Factors' market. The company opened branches in New York in 1994 and in Hong Kong in 1995. As the domestic apparel, furniture, and textile markets have matured, First Factors International was established to offer export and import factoring services. Management is particularly excited about the potential of Asia, and in 1996 the company allied itself with First Union Bank, an Indonesian bank, and a mainland China trading company to provide financial services to Asian companies who want to sell their products in America.

Those Asian companies are in much the same position that the English exporters were 250 years ago. They face great opportunities, but considerable risk, in going into the American market. A relationship with First Factors International enables them to reduce the risk and maximize the opportunity. The factoring company investigates the credit standing of potential buyers of the Asian-made products, assumes the credit risk, handles collections, and advances the Asian client funds in advance of collection. The export company is assured of immediate operating capital and can devote its energy to manufacturing and marketing, while leaving the burdens of credit and collection management to the factor. ∞

The First Factors Building in downtown High Point

The First Factors Corporation Team, 1996

Aerial view of downtown High Point in the 1970s. *Photo courtesy The High Point Museum Archives.*

Robert G. Culp Jr. spent much of his career as a highly placed, successful sales executive for a fabric company. When he was in his mid-50s, he embarked on a new venture. In 1972, when both the national economy and the textile industry were in the midst of a deep recession, he used his life savings to start a fabric company. He proved to be the consummate entrepreneur. The history of Culp, Inc. is a series of decisions that flew in the face of conventional wisdom, and a story of the living out of Bob Culp's vision.

Culp began with three employees: Howard Dunn Jr., who is now the company president; Frances Elliott, who has since retired; and R. G. "Rob" Culp Jr., now chairman and chief executive officer. At first, the company bought fabric and resold it to small and medium-sized furniture companies.

Today, Culp, Inc. manufactures and markets a full line of upholstery and ticking fabrics, and is the only company to do so. Industry wisdom says "do one thing and do it well." R. G. Culp said, "Get into every fabric and all markets, and protect yourself from being wiped out when, for instance, velvet cycles out of popularity or van conversions take a nosedive." His idea was that not all markets would be down at the same time.

Before R. G. Culp's death in 1991, the company had manufacturing facilities in Burlington, Stokesdale, and Graham, North Carolina, and Anderson and Pageland, South Carolina. Warehouse and distribution centers were located near the major furniture centers, in High Point, Mississippi, and California.

Long before exceptional customer service became a key competitive strategy, R. G. Culp was determined not only to satisfy, but also to delight the customer. Upholstery companies generally preferred long mill runs and weren't inclined to upset production schedules to accommodate customers. Culp's philosophy was to give the customer what he or she wanted.

A charismatic leader who was respected and loved by his employees, Culp set the example for going the "extra mile." Even after

Robert G. Culp Jr.

he retired, he was in the office every day, generating hundreds of ideas, "going at 110 mph." He had little use for hierarchy, bureaucracy, or formality. For example, employee phone lists have always been arranged alphabetically—by first name. No parking spaces have ever been reserved for top brass. Culp's theory was that the person who got to work first deserved the best space, whether that was the janitor or the CEO.

Culp was a believer that "what gets you in trouble in bad times are decisions you made in good times." While textile plants all over the country were closing, Culp, Inc. has never had to close a plant. When operations were acquired from other companies, the Culp culture took hold quickly. Employees refer to the process as "Culpmatization"— and describe it as a combination of respect for all employees, high expectations, a

willingness to turn the world upside down to please a customer, and a strong commitment to ethical behavior.

In the 1990s, Culp, Inc. has acquired manufacturing operations in Georgia, Pennsylvania, and Quebec, and has made a major commitment to furthering another of the founder's visionary ideas—global expansion. The company is aggressively seeking out worldwide business opportunities, including acquisitions, joint ventures, and sourcing of raw materials.

A publicly traded company, Culp has some 3,000 employees in 1996, and net sales of $308 million in fiscal 1995. ☙

Classic Gallery Group

In late 1972, Charlie Greene and a group of associates began examining the furniture industry and formulating plans for a new business. From those discussions and plans, Classic Gallery was born.

Opening in February, 1973, and founded on the principles of quality workmanship and materials, Classic Gallery produced contemporary upholstered furniture targeted for interior design showrooms. Greene attributes the company's immediate success and steady growth to its employees, especially the original 15 skilled workers. By 1996, 23 years later, 3 of the 15 had retired, 4 had left the company for other employment, and an amazing 8 were still on board.

Rather than go after the business of large furniture chains and department stores, Classic Gallery chose to concentrate on specialty orders for design showrooms and small shops. "We build custom-made furniture," Greene said.

Some of those orders have included an extra long sofa for a 7'2" professional basketball player, extra strong furniture for a professional football player, and special seating for the luxury yachts of dignitaries like Jordan's King Hussein. Others who come home to Classic Gallery seating include Vice President and Mrs. Al Gore and former President and Mrs. Gerald Ford. When a

Charlie Greene, Classic Gallery Group

new Radisson Hotel was built in downtown High Point, the furniture capital of the world, Classic Gallery was selected to make the seating.

The company has grown over the years to include Ecco Designs, a glass and metal company started in 1980, and Classic Traditions, a traditional upholstered furniture line formally known as Earlon, acquired in 1985.

Classic Gallery's market strength remains its flexibility and quality. Basic designs can be scaled up or down to work in an intimate residential setting or a large hotel ballroom. Most of the pieces are custom built, and half of the upholstery fabrics are sent in by customers for their orders.

The background of the company's founder is equally interesting. For Charlie Greene, it was computer expertise that led to the furniture industry. A native of New Jersey, Greene was trained in electronics in the Air Force, which led to work with the Winston-Salem office of Dun & Bradstreet when his time in the service ended.

From D&B, Greene joined an associate installing a new computer system for a High Point upholstery manufacturer, KayLyn, Inc., in 1966. As the installation neared completion, the company offered him a job as data processing manager, and his career in the furniture industry was underway.

In 1967, after a year of exposure to the marketing and manufacturing sides of the business, Greene was appointed general manager of another KayLyn division. In 1972 he left to form Classic Gallery.

Classic Gallery Group Showroom, High Point, North Carolina

Since making High Point his home, Charlie Greene has been one its most active community volunteers, serving as chairman of the Chamber of Commerce, the High Point Education Foundation, and the board of Guilford Technical Community College. He has served as president of the Southern Furniture Club, and on the boards of High Point Regional Hospital, Maryfield Nursing Home, and the national board of the American Society of Interior Designers. He was honored as High Point's Citizen of the Year in 1990.

The company that didn't want to be just another furniture company has prospered by specializing in giving customers exactly what they want and delivering it on time. Offering more options than are available in most lines of furniture has been good for growth. The Classic Gallery Group now has 65 employees working in more than 100,000 square feet of manufacturing space on Fulton Place in High Point. ∞

In July of 1976, Jim Stewart of Cambridge Corp. and Coy Williard of Decorative Sales & Service, Inc. combined their experience and talents to form what was later to be known as Williard-Stewart, Inc. Their partnership began by offering building and remodeling services to established customers, while building and remodeling showrooms in High Point, as well as in Dallas and Atlanta during the years those cities had large furniture markets. Showroom designers who worked with Williard-Stewart in High Point found it easier and more efficient to bring the company to Dallas and Atlanta than to work with unfamiliar contractors. Meeting designers and furniture officials in Dallas and Atlanta also created new opportunities in High Point.

Today, furniture showrooms constitute less than 50 percent of the business, with the balance in single family homes, commercial buildings, warehouses, and apartments. In 1996 Williard-Stewart developed one housing subdivision with plans for a second subdivision. Unlike most general contractors, the company handles most of the work itself, subcontracting plumbing, electrical, heating, and air-conditioning.

What makes Williard-Stewart highly unusual in the general contracting field is that the 50-plus people who work for the company are full-time, year-round employees. Unlike most employees in the construction trade, they receive group insurance, 401-K plans, paid holidays, and vacations. Keeping carpenters and painters busy through the winter is a challenge this company has met year in and year out.

In order to provide millwork in a timely manner, Williard-Stewart incorporated Woodmasters of High Point in early 1983. Woodmasters is a millshop specializing in doors, windows, mantels, and showroom props, as well as kitchen cabinets that are used in residential construction.

What began as two diverse companies has evolved into a full-service company providing general construction, painting, wall and floor covering, and millwork. Since 1991, these companies have been housed in the old Crown Hosiery building at 449 South Wrenn Street. The remodeled building is a showcase for the wall coverings, floor coverings, furniture, windows, doors, and construction techniques that Williard-Stewart offers to its customers.

Williard and Stewart attribute their company's success to hiring and retaining excellent employees. They remember being "on the other side," and endeavor to make sure that Williard-Stewart employees, an understandably loyal and stable group, have what most construction workers don't—financial stability, air-conditioned comfort in the millshop and vans, and a voice in the operations through weekly staff meetings. It has been very satisfying for them to see their employees advance and prosper. ∞

The Williard-Stewart team

Phillips Mills, Inc.

Phillips Mills grew out of Phillips-Davis, Inc., a selling agent and converter of upholstery fabrics which was founded in 1932 by Earl N. Phillips and his uncle, W. Stanley Davis. Phillips had been a salesman for DuPont in Virginia, and he moved to High Point to establish his own business to sell upholstery materials to the furniture industry.

Soon after Earl Phillips died in 1975, his son, Stanley Davis "Dave" Phillips, became president and began to vertically expand the company. Over the next few years, Phillips Weaving Mills, Phillips Velvet Mills, and Phillips Printing Mills were established, and in 1979 the corporate name was changed to Phillips Mills, Inc.

During this time, Phillips Mills has grown to be one of the largest upholstery fabric manufacturers. The latest technology is used in its operations, including computerized design systems and production equipment.

Much of the company's recent growth has been in the international arena. Phillips Mills' products are sold in Europe, Asia, Africa, and both the Middle East and Far East. International business now accounts for 25 percent of sales.

The company is a subsidiary of Phillips Industries, of which Dave Phillips is the chief executive officer. He now spends much of his time in the state capital and traveling abroad as North Carolina's Secretary of Commerce. Choosing Mr. Phillips for that position was the first appointment James Hunt made when he was elected governor of North Carolina in 1992.

The officers of the Phillips textile group are Pete Thompson, vice president—Administration; Lawry Bump, vice president— Sales; Larry Lewis, secretary/treasurer; Susan Delong, vice president—Design; Bill Asbill, vice president—Velvet; Dave Stewart, vice president—Weaving; and Stan Cathell, vice president—Printing. ∽

Seated: Susan DeLong, vice president—Design; S. Davis Phillips, president; Larry N. Lewis, secretary/treasurer; *Standing:* Peter C. Thompson, vice president—Administration; Lawrence W. Bump, vice president—Sales; William C. Asbill, vice president/general manager—Velvet; Dave Stewart, vice president/general manager—Weaving

Factoring has always been an
important service to the furniture
industry, and in 1957 Earl N. Phillips
established Factors, Inc. as a subsidiary
of his upholstery sales company,
Phillips-Davis, Inc.

Factors, Inc. was sold to NCNB
(now NationsBank) in 1970, and
another company, First Factors, Inc.
was soon started as a subsidiary of
Phillips-Davis, Inc. The founders
were: E. N. Phillips, Phil Phillips,
Dave Phillips, J. E. Foscue, W. M.
Webster, and William Crews.
Approximately a decade later, a third
factoring company, Phillips Factors
Corporation, was created as a subsidiary of Phillips Industries, Inc. (suc-
cessor to Phillips-Davis). The founders
were Robert Niebauer, William Crews,
and Dave Phillips.

The furniture industry remains a
focus of this rapidly growing company,
which also provides factoring and
other financial services to other manufacturing and service industries, both
nationally and internationally.

In 1987, Phillips Financial
Corporation was begun as a subsidiary
of Phillips Factors Corporation. This
company provides accounts receivable
management and financial support for
service industries.

Dave Phillips serves as chairman with Bob
Niebauer as president of Phillips Factors
Corporation and Mitch Wiggs as president of
Phillips Financial Corporation.

Phillips Industries Inc. and its subsidiary
companies support the High Point community through gifts and through volunteer
leadership in many local endeavors. The
largest beneficiary of the company's philanthropy is the Lillian J. Phillips Cancer
Pavilion at High Point Regional Hospital.
The company supports numerous charitable
organizations including educational and civic
groups. ∞

Left to right: Robert C. Niebauer, S. Davis Phillips

For almost a century, 305 West High Street has been an address that faces the future.

In 1902 S. H. Tomlinson started building Tomlinson Chair Manufacturing Co. Today it is the oldest surviving furniture factory site in the city. In 1924 Tomlinson and his brother, C.F., built a showroom and office building. Together these buildings contained 500,000 square feet, and as many as 900 people were employed there.

One of the most respected names in furniture manufacturing, Tomlinson was the first of the High Point companies to show its goods in northern markets, the first to advertise and market nationally, and to introduce a totally coordinated group of furniture. For more than half a century, many of High Point's most skilled craftsmen learned their craft at Tomlinson, during a period when no formal training programs existed.

In the early 1970s, S. Davis Phillips and Dick Behrends optioned the Tomlinson property for showroom use, and introduced the name "Market Square." This option was not exercised; however, in the late 1970s after a reorganization, Tomlinson was purchased by Jake Froelich, Charles Haywood, and their wives. In 1981 an investor group including Froelich, Haywood, Phillips, and George Lyles Jr. began the purchase of these historic buildings and started renovating them for showrooms for high-end home furnishings, accessories, and rugs. The first phase of Market Square opened for the spring 1982 furniture market. Unlike most showrooms in High Point, these are open to the trade all year round.

The renovation of the rest of the buildings was completed for use in 1984. Included was 100,000 square feet for trade shows, temporary exhibits, and food service for up to 1,300 people. Pat Plaxico, ASID, provided design for all of the projects.

The Market Square complex continued to grow with the acquisition of the Holiday Inn and Furniture Plaza Buildings on Main Street and the Hamilton Market Building. A Howard Johnson Hotel and Carolina Atlantic Film Studio were added in 1985.

The growth of Market Square parallels the increasing consolidation of the furniture market.

Rounding out a decade of innovative development, the owners of Market Square opened Market Square Tower in 1990. The new 15-story building was sensitively designed to complement its historic neighbors, to which it is connected. The tower was the first mixed-use building constructed in North Carolina, containing showrooms, office space, and residential condominiums. It is the center for Showtime, the international textile show in January and July.

Market Square general partners George Lyles Jr. and Dave Phillips, and managing general partner Jake Froelich own the three condominiums on the 15th floor—a good place to view how their vision was translated into this exciting complex.

An appraiser of the old Tomlinson buildings during reorganization in the 1970s recommended that they be torn down. But Froelich, Lyles, and Phillips saw that the old brick, many windows, maple and oak floors, and massive ceiling beams had quality and character worth preserving. Now Market Square is the largest building in North Carolina and the sixth largest in the United States to be listed on the National Register of Historic Places. Historic features create a warm atmosphere for the showrooms and give a distinctive charm to eating and meeting places in the complex, including the String and Splinter Club in the old executive office space of Tomlinson Manufacturing, and the Boiler Room Bar and Restaurant in the underground factory boiler room. ∞

Market Square Design Center

Market Square Textile Tower

The Radisson Hotel High Point opened in October 1983. It offers exceptional facilities and a staff that pride themselves on providing quality service. The hotel is conveniently located in central North Carolina in downtown High Point, the "Home Furnishings Capital of the World." Adjacent to the International Home Furnishings Center on Highway 311, the Radisson is within easy access to Interstates 40 and 85. Business, shopping, and entertainment are nearby as well as the Piedmont Triad International Airport.

The facility offers 251 guest rooms and suites and a Business Class Level featuring added privacy and special amenities and services. The hotel is fully accessible to the disabled and provides non-smoking rooms upon availability. Each room is equipped with remote-cable television, AM/FM clock radio, voice- mail message telephone, desk, and valet laundry service.

With more than 12,000 square feet of meeting space, the property provides the finest in flexible, contemporary facilities for conventions, business meetings, and social events. The 5,100-square-foot ballroom can be divided into four separate salons for smaller groups and is ideal for large meetings or social gatherings. In addition, there is an upscale board room located on the second floor that can accommodate a meeting of up to 20 people. From a simple coffee break to a lavish banquet, the Radisson's team of professionals delivers courteous and responsive service to ensure the successful execution of every function.

You may enjoy a variety of delicious American cuisine in the restaurant or relax in the lounge for quiet conversation and cocktails. The restaurant and lounge are noted for their distinctive culinary excellence and they are enhanced by an atmosphere of simple elegance overlooking a spacious lobby.

For your recreational pleasure, health club facilities are available including an indoor pool, Jacuzzi™, and exercise equipment. The hotel is also close to many fine public golf courses, tennis courts, and lakes for fishing, skiing, and boating.

High Point and the surrounding area offer visitors a variety of interesting activities, events, and attractions.

The Radisson welcomes you and looks forward to being your "home away from home" as it consistently strives to exceed your expectations for a pleasant and memorable stay. ⌘

Atlantic Photographics, Inc.

"Are we staged and ready in Bay 10? The merchandise is here for the room-scene in Bay 5. Job 9512 is a digital shot. Set 8 is a rip."

When Jim Hulin and John Raines opened the doors of Atlantic Photographics, Inc. (API) on January 1, 1984, they only dreamed of the hustle and bustle of today's thriving commercial photography studio.

Their first studio location on East Kivett Drive employed a staff of four, including the two owners as the photographers. Both had been employed as commercial photographers in local studios. They knew the market, had the skill, and possessed the determination to create a different kind of studio.

Their dream was simple. Beyond the business basics of quality control and profitability, they wanted to create an enjoyable place to work and grow. And while that goal may sound clichéd, they set out to make it a day-to-day reality. They ran their business with hard work, strong ethics, and a desire to maintain a balance in life between work and family time.

Those founding principles are still evident at today's API. After 12 years in the business, API employs approximately 40 people who meet the demanding daily deadlines of the photography business in an atmosphere of hard work and camaraderie.

The commercial photography industry has prospered in the High Point area as a vital support to the home furnishings industries. From furniture to accessories to textiles, industry manufacturers require quality photography to sell their products to retail buyers and the consuming public.

Manufacturers from around the country choose to have their photographic work done at API because of the expertise and proximity to their primary showroom locations here in "the furniture capital of the world."

Atlantic Photographics' client list also includes many manufacturers and retailers outside the home furnishings industry. From

Jim Hulin (L) and John Raines (R) utilize the age-less traditional view camera and the new-age digital camera system.

high-tech aerospace equipment to hardware, from exquisite jewelry to vending machines, if a photographic image can help it sell, Atlantic will provide the quality images.

Recent enhancements in photographic imaging technology have led to the formation of a new Imaging Services Division of API. "We've watched the steady advancements in technology and quality over the last few years," explains John Raines, president of the company. "Finally the level of quality is there to meet our standards and our customers' needs."

"This new system gives us the ability to streamline the traditional photographic and retouching processes to give our clients more choices and a quality product with the pinpoint accuracy and control of the computer."

It's a long way from the early days of their respective photographic careers, but these two dedicated businessmen continue to make tough decisions without straying from their core philosophies.

"We're eager to continue providing our customers a quality photographic product with a view to the future," Jim Hulin states.

"But we never forget who we are and why we started our business years ago. We're grateful to our many customers for our success, and we're proud of the atmosphere within our company. We've got a great group of employees." ∞

Bibliography

Corbitt, David Leroy. *The Formation of the North Carolina Counties. 1663-1943.* Raleigh, North Carolina: State Department of Archives and History, 1950.

Hicks, Robert F., Jr. "Spirit of Enterprise: The History of High Point's Formative Period, 1851-1926." Master's thesis, University of North Carolina at Greensboro, 1989.

High Point Chamber of Commerce. *The Building and the Builders of a City.* High Point, North Carolina, 1947.

Hinshaw, Seth B., and Mary Edith, ed., *Carolina Quakers: Our Heritage of Hope. Tercentenary 1672-1972.* Greensboro, North Carolina: North Carolina Yearly Meeting, 1972.

McPherson, Holt. *High Pointers of High Point.* High Point, North Carolina: High Point Chamber of Commerce, 1976.

Rights, Douglas L. *The American Indian in North Carolina.* Winston-Salem, North Carolina: John F. Blair, 1957.

Robinson, Blackwell P., and Alexander R. Stoesen. *History of Guilford County, North Carolina.* Greensboro, North Carolina: Project of the Guilford County Bicentennial Commission, 1971 and the Guilford County American Revolution Bicentennial Commission, 1976.

Sharpe, Bill. *A New Geography of North Carolina.* Vol. 2. Raleigh, North Carolina: Sharpe Publishing Co., Inc., 1958.

Shipman, Roy, comp. *High Point. A Pictorial History 1859-1983.* High Point, North Carolina: Hall Printing Co., 1983.

Smith, H. McKelden, ed., *Architectural Resources. High Point, Jamestown, Gibsonville, Guilford County, North Carolina.* Raleigh, North Carolina: North Carolina Department of Cultural Resources, Division of Archives and History, 1979.

Thomas, David Nolan. *Early History of the North Carolina Furniture Industry, 1880-1921.* Ann Arbor, Michigan: University Microfilms, 1964.

Wetmore, Ruth Y. *First On the Land: The North Carolina Indians.* Winston-Salem: John F. Blair, 1975.

Acknowledgements

The following provided specific assistance, support, and encouragement in the development of
High Point: Reflections of the Past.

Executive Director Sherri Simon and staff of The High Point Museum & Historical Park: John Marks, Jane Willis, Jerri Barbour, and John Moseley

Mary Lib (Mrs. Fred) Clark Joyce for The Historical Collection of Stephen C. Clark

City of High Point clerk's office; Department of Planning and Development

High Point Economic Development Corporation

High Point Chamber of Commerce

High Point Convention & Visitors Bureau

Neal F. Austin High Point Public Library

Greensboro Public Library

Jamestown Public Library

International Home Furnishings Center

International Home Furnishings Marketing Association

High Point Enterprise

Greensboro News & Record

First United Methodist Church: Robert B. Rankin

Mrs. Sanders Dallas

Mrs. W. G. Ragsdale

Rachel Gray

Joe Patterson

Henry Dowdy

George Lyles Jr.

Forrest and Judy Cates

B'Nai Israel Synagogue: Rabbi Tamara Miller

Peggy Wainer

Sylvia Silver

Fred Swartzberg

Jake Harris

The editor wishes to thank Robert Hicks for agreeing to serve as editorial consultant for the book.

High Point's Enterprises

Patrons

B B & T

Odom & Company

Index

"Jack the Fire Dog" was adopted by the High Point
Fire Department and accompanied the firefighters
on calls during the 1920s.

OUR WEDDING ALBUM

A Memory Book

Celebrating the marriage

of _____

and _____

Illustrated by Beshlie • Designed by Doug Bergstreser

Viking Studio Books
First American Edition. Published in 1992 by Viking Penguin,
a division of Penguin Books USA Inc., 375 Hudson Street, New York, New York 10014
Illustrations © 1992 by Gallery Five. Copyright © 1992 by Intervisual Books, Inc.,
Los Angeles, California 90045   IBI: 193-07   ISBN 0-670-84594-9   Printed and bound in Singapore
1 3 5 7 9 10 8 6 4 2

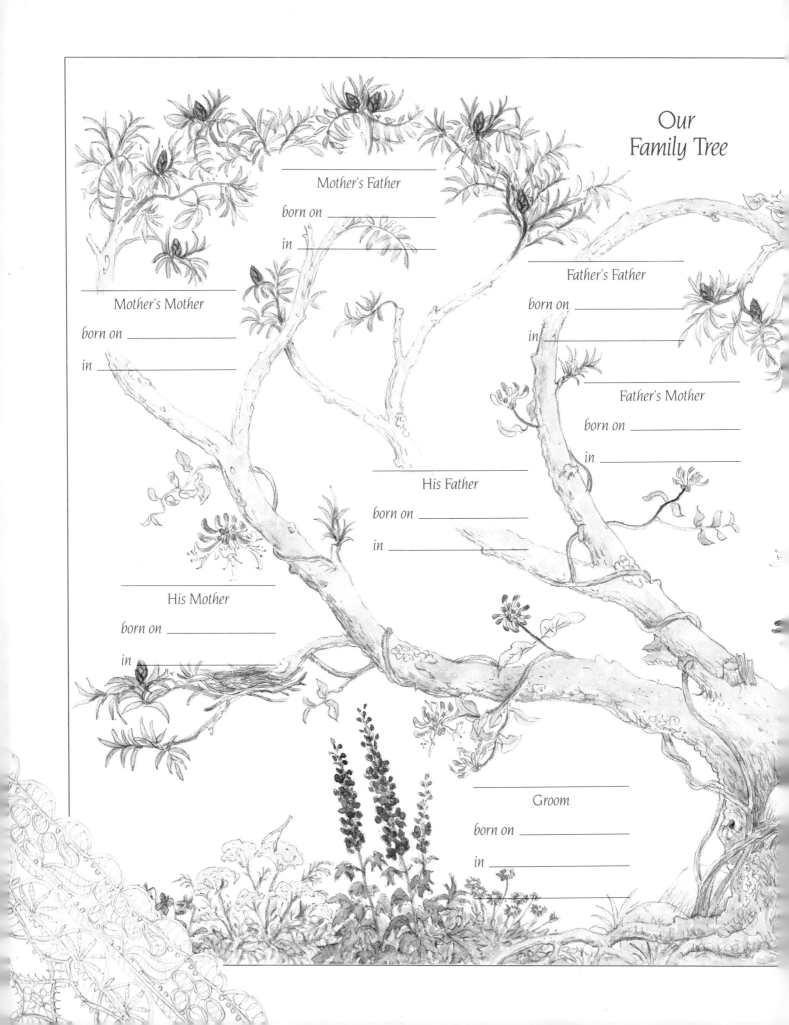

Our
Family Tree

Mother's Father

born on _____

in _____

Father's Father

born on _____

in _____

Mother's Mother

born on _____

in _____

Father's Mother

born on _____

in _____

His Father

born on _____

in _____

His Mother

born on _____

in _____

Groom

born on _____

in _____

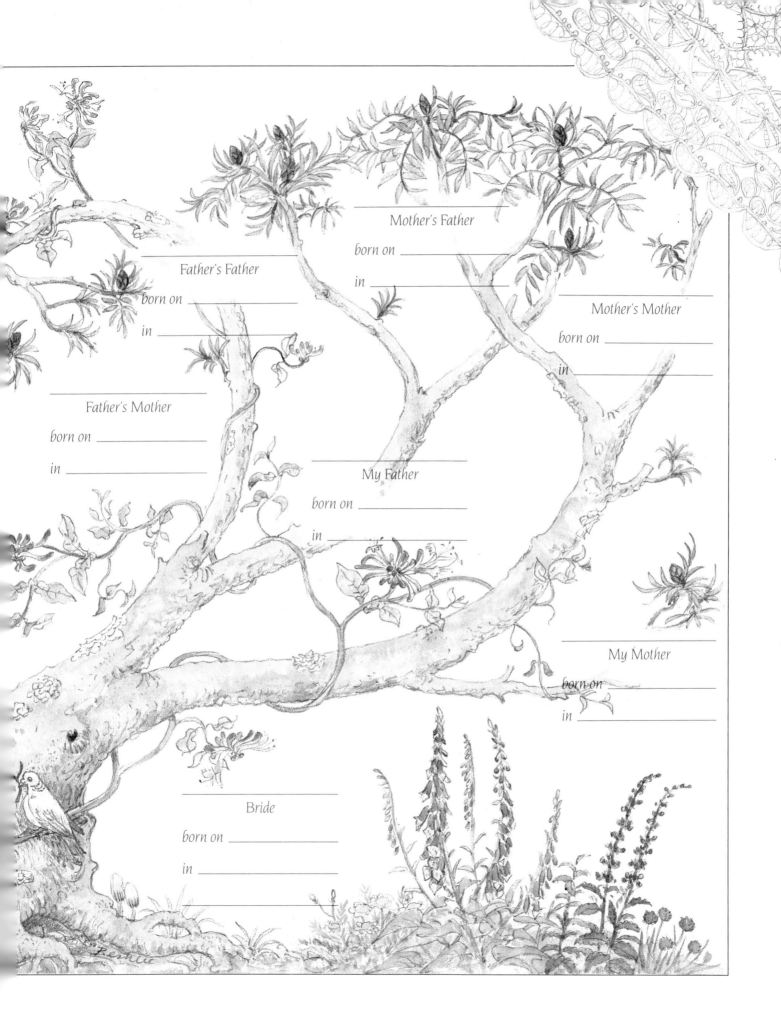

Mother's Father

born on _____

in _____

Father's Father

born on _____

in _____

Mother's Mother

born on _____

in _____

Father's Mother

born on _____

in _____

My Father

born on _____

in _____

My Mother

born on _____

in _____

Bride

born on _____

in _____

How We Met

The day we first met was _____

_____

_____

We first met at _____

_____

_____

We were introduced by _____

My first impressions of him _____

_____

_____

_____

My first impressions of her _____

_____

_____

_____

What attracted me to him _____

_____

_____

What attracted me to her _____

_____

_____

Something unique I noticed about him _____

_____

Something unique I noticed about her _____

_____

Our Courtship

Our first date _____

_____

What we did _____

_____

Our first kiss _____

_____

Our funniest date _____

_____

_____

Our most romantic evening _____

_____

_____

_____

We first knew we were in love when _____

_____

_____

_____

Place a
courtship photograph
here.

The first time I met his parents _____

_____

_____

_____

The first time I met her parents _____

_____

_____

_____

The Proposal

Where it happened and when _____

_____

I prepared before proposing by _____

_____

_____

It came about _____

_____

_____

I said _____

_____

_____

The reply _____

_____

We picked out the ring _____

_____

We celebrated our decision to marry by _____

_____

_____

_____

Each of us thought life would change after marriage by _____

_____

_____

_____

_____

Our Engagement

We first told _____

We told our parents _____

_____

_____

Their reactions _____

_____

_____

We told our friends _____

_____

_____

Their reactions _____

_____

_____

Engagement parties in our honor _____

_____

_____

_____

_____

_____

Place your engagement portrait here.

How we felt during our engagement _____

_____

_____

_____

_____

_____

_____

_____

Planning for Our Wedding

I chose my dress _____

_____

_____

The bridesmaids will wear _____

_____

The ushers will wear _____

_____

The Wedding Party

Bridesmaids   Ushers

_____   _____

_____   _____

_____   _____

_____   _____

_____   _____

Choosing the guest list was _____

_____

Addressing our invitations _____

_____

_____

We picked out our cake _____

Flowers and colors we chose _____

The ceremony and reception will be held at _____

_____

Who helped us the most _____

_____

Bridal Registries and Showers

Where we registered _____

Different patterns we chose

_____   _____

_____   _____

_____   _____

The hardest thing about picking patterns was _____

_____

_____

Showers were given by _____

_____

Who attended

_____   _____   _____

_____   _____   _____

_____   _____   _____

_____   _____   _____

_____   _____   _____

_____   _____   _____

_____   _____   _____

The funniest gift was _____

_____

_____

The most memorable gift was _____

_____

_____

Parties

The Bachelor Party

Where and when _____

_____

They did _____

_____

It lasted until _____

The funniest thing someone did was _____

_____

Gag gifts _____

_____

His most embarrassing moment _____

_____

The Bachelorette Party

Where and when _____

_____

We did _____

_____

It lasted until _____

The funniest thing someone did was _____

_____

Gag gifts _____

_____

Her most embarrassing moment _____

_____

_____

The Wedding Rehearsal and Dinner

When _____

Who was there _____

_____

What went wrong _____

_____

What went right _____

_____

The best advice given to calm us was _____

_____

Some things still weren't ready _____

_____

_____

The dinner was held at _____

Toasts made _____

_____

_____

_____

_____

Funniest moment _____

_____

_____

_____

The gifts we gave to the wedding party were _____

_____

_____

Place a
rehearsal photograph
here.

Our Wedding Day

We each woke up at _____

The first things we did were _____

_____

_____

_____

Our first thoughts were _____

_____

_____

_____

The bride was so nervous, she couldn't _____

_____

_____

The groom was so nervous, he couldn't _____

_____

_____

Last minute details that still weren't ready _____

_____

_____

Who helped the bride get ready _____

_____

Who helped the groom get ready _____

_____

The bride left for the ceremony at _____

The groom left for the ceremony at _____

The last and best bits of advice were _____

_____

_____

Our parents said to us _____

_____

_____

To calm ourselves, we _____

_____

The bride's something old _____

       something new _____

       something borrowed _____

       something blue _____

Traditions we kept _____

_____

The weather was _____

_____

_____

Final thoughts before the ceremony _____

Place a
wedding photograph
here.

_____

_____

_____

_____

_____

_____

The Ceremony

Who performed it _____

_____

The bride was escorted down the aisle by _____

_____

The music was _____

_____

Our vows were _____

_____

_____

_____

_____

The most important part of the vows to him _____

_____

_____

_____

The most important part of the vows to her _____

_____

_____

_____

During the ceremony, we thought _____

_____

_____

_____

_____

Wedding Guests

_____   _____   _____

_____   _____   _____

_____   _____   _____

_____   _____   _____

_____   _____   _____

_____   _____   _____

_____   _____   _____

_____   _____   _____

_____   _____   _____

_____   _____   _____

_____   _____   _____

_____   _____   _____

_____   _____   _____

_____   _____   _____

Place
wedding day mementos
and additional guest lists
here.

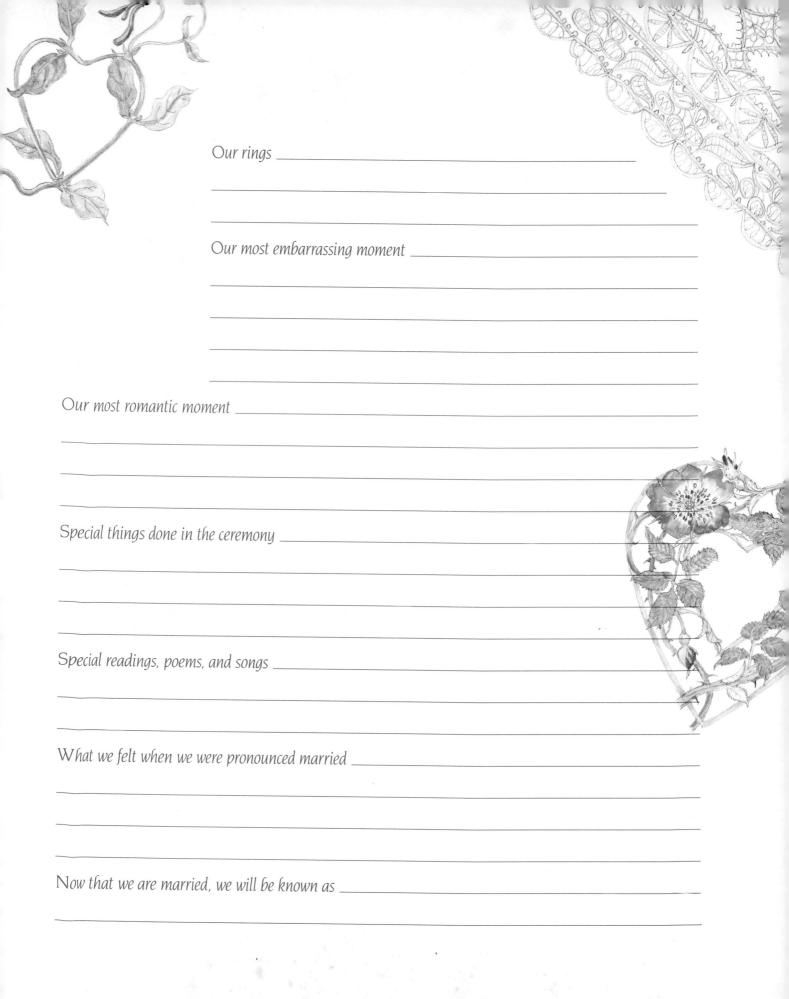

Our rings _____

_____

_____

Our most embarrassing moment _____

_____

_____

_____

_____

Our most romantic moment _____

_____

_____

_____

Special things done in the ceremony _____

_____

_____

_____

Special readings, poems, and songs _____

_____

_____

What we felt when we were pronounced married _____

_____

_____

_____

Now that we are married, we will be known as _____

_____

Wedding Gifts

Gift	From Whom	Thank-you Sent
_____	_____	_____
_____	_____	_____
_____	_____	_____
_____	_____	_____
_____	_____	_____
_____	_____	_____
_____	_____	_____
_____	_____	_____
_____	_____	_____
_____	_____	_____
_____	_____	_____
_____	_____	_____
_____	_____	_____
_____	_____	_____
_____	_____	_____
_____	_____	_____
_____	_____	_____
_____	_____	_____

We opened our gifts at _____

_____

Our most memorable gift was _____

_____

_____

The Reception

It was held at _____
_____

We got there by _____
_____

It lasted until _____

We served _____
_____
_____

Our first dance was _____
_____

Our music was _____
_____
_____

The first toast was _____
_____
_____
_____
_____

The funniest toast was _____
_____
_____
_____
_____
_____
_____

Place a
reception photograph
here.

Some funny things that happened that first year were _____

_____

_____

_____

_____

Our first holiday as husband and wife was _____

_____

_____

_____

Our favorite pastimes were _____

_____

The first time our in-laws came to dinner was _____

_____

_____

_____

Our silliest disagreement was _____

_____

_____

New traditions we started _____

_____

_____

Some funny stories about fixing up our new home _____

_____

_____

_____

Our First Anniversary

We celebrated at _____

We celebrated by _____

_____

We gave one another _____

_____

Thoughts about our first year together _____

_____

_____

Marriage has changed our lives by _____

_____

_____

Our love has changed by _____

_____

_____

We're different now because _____

_____

We've learned from one another that _____

_____

_____

Some new things in our life are _____

_____

Our one-year-old cake tasted like _____

If we had to do it over, we would _____

_____

_____